Tarzan

OF THE APES

Tarzan

OF THE APES

BY BURNE HOGARTH

Original text by Edgar Rice Burroughs
adapted by Robert M. Hodes

Introduction by Maurice Horn

WATSON-GUPTILL PUBLICATIONS/NEW YORK

I remember a day long ago when
I was twelve. My father, with a
bundle tucked under his arm,
took me on a long street car ride
to the Art Institute of Chicago,
and there, unrolling a pile of my
drawings, sketches and scraps he
had carefully saved, asked the
men at the desk if these were
sufficient reason to let me enroll
in the school's Saturday classes.
That's how it all started.

I give this book back to my father.
He would have been proud to see
these pages.

Copyright © 1972 by Edgar Rice Burroughs, Inc.
First published 1972 in New York by Watson-Guptill Publications,
a division of Billboard Publications, Inc.,
165 West 46 Street, New York, N.Y.

Manufactured in U.S.A.

First Printing, 1972

Library of Congress Cataloging in Publication Data
Hogarth, Burne.
    Edgar Rice Burroughs' Tarzan of the apes.

    Bibliography: p.
    I. Burroughs, Edgar Rice, 1875–1950.   Tarzan of the
apes.   II. Title: Tarzan of the apes.
NC1429.H553A44   741.59'73   72–2446
ISBN 0–8230–5060–2

This new pictorial version of *Tarzan of the Apes,* based on the famous novel by Edgar Rice Burroughs, could be called with equal justification *The Return of Hogarth.*

It has been more than twenty years since Burne Hogarth drew his last "Tarzan" page in August, 1950, but the images he created live on. When Hogarth gave up the strip, he thought he was closing the book on his past. But as a comic strip artist he had made a lasting impact; no one else ever created such a void after his departure. Time and time again Hogarth was asked to come back to "Tarzan." He declined—until he finally succumbed to the entreaties of his admirers and agreed to illustrate the present version of *Tarzan of the Apes.*

In this introduction, I shall try to elucidate—with Hogarth's own words and with quotations from the writings of others—the unique power and artistry of the man who endowed Tarzan with such charisma and visual splendor.

When I wrote the introduction for *Tarzan, Seigneur de la Jungle* (Paris: Azur, 1967), this, in abbreviated form, is what I had to say about Hogarth and his work:

In the course of an extraordinary career extending over more than forty years, Burne Hogarth has covered the entire range of artistic fields; he has been illustrator, cartoonist, engraver, teacher, school founder, art theorist, painter, and writer. In all these disciplines, Hogarth has left his personal mark; in all of them he has succeeded and, at times, excelled. If he has gone from one mode of expression to another, relentlessly starting afresh, relentlessly experimenting, his career did not reflect discouragement or failure, but the will to proceed ever further: "to forever push on," as André Gide recommended. To understand Hogarth's work and its scope, it is necessary to follow its development step by step.

Burne Hogarth was born on Christmas Day, 1911, in Chicago. He displayed artistic inclinations as a child and later studied art history and anthropology at Crane College and Northwestern University in Chicago, then at Columbia University in New York. He learned to draw, however, at the Chicago Art Institute, the breeding ground of so many American artists.

At the age of fifteen, he became an assistant cartoonist at Associated Editors Syndicate, while pursuing his studies at the same time. He was not yet sixteen when the syndicate asked him to draw his own feature, "Famous Churches of the World," and to illustrate two sports features. In 1929—he was eighteen—he created, for Bonnet-Brown Company, his first comic strip, "Ivy Hemmanhaw," which met with little success. Changing syndicate and genre, he published a feature panel the following year entitled "Odd Occupations and Strange Accidents" for Leeds Features.

A little later, in 1933, he taught art history for the WPA (Works Progress Administration), one of the agencies set up by President Roosevelt to palliate the increasingly severe effects of the depression which had struck the United States in 1929. In spite of the satisfaction that teaching gave him, Hogarth dreamt only of drawing and, in 1934, he went to try his luck in New York, the only place where a cartoonist could get his talent recognized. After a few months spent as an assistant in the studios of King Features Syndicate, Hogarth was given a chance by MacNaught Syndicate.

In 1935, he took over "Pieces of Eight," a pirate story penned by Charles Driscoll. Although Hogarth's style was still awkward, the first elements of his particular universe are already to be found in the jagged branches on which slimy moss grows and in the tormented landscapes of threatening forms.

But it was in 1936 that Hogarth could at last give his all. After Hal Foster had announced his decision to leave "Tarzan," which he had been drawing for United Feature Syndicate since 1929, Hogarth, among many others, applied for Foster's place. He was accepted at first try on the strength of the sample drawing he had submitted.

When Burne Hogarth undertook the assignment to draw "Tarzan," the Lord of the Jungle had already been in existence for twenty-two years in the novels of Edgar Rice Burroughs; he had been a character in the movies for eighteen years; he had been a comic strip hero for eight. If the themes of Tarzan had followed a definite tradition—a dream Africa, a mythical jungle, warlike tribes, lost cities, exoticism—Hogarth, while remaining outwardly faithful to these themes, gave them a much more authentic quality of strangeness, a quality reflecting the strangeness of Hogarth's own vision and style.

This famous style—recognizable among all others—was at first derivative of Foster's, but it was not long before it started changing. Into "Tarzan" Hogarth poured his entire artistic culture: his admiration for Michelangelo and the great baroque artists, his affinities with German expressionism, and his knowledge of the arts of the East.

From that moment on, Tarzan's universe becomes a world of bristling, sharp forms curving upon themselves: pinnacles of lava around volcanoes, razor-sharp peaks on the horizon, claws and beaks of birds of prey, long and pointed leaves, and deformed and exaggerated horns and tusks. The fundamental motifs of the curve and point are everywhere present. The action is completely imbued with a tragic quality which shows particularly in the faces, tormented with passion or hatred. In "Tarzan" all Hogarth's esthetic ideas are translated into visual forms.

In his desire to fuse form and content ever more closely, Hogarth developed the art of composition to an almost exaggerated degree of exactitude, not for the sake of arbitrary virtuosity, but in answer to the demands of the subject and the narrative. Each of his pages could stand on its own, but their succession brings to light, step by step, a universe of menacing foliage and tentacular roots into which Tarzan enters as on a field of arms.

A work of singular genius, Hogarth's "Tarzan" marks one of the supreme moments of the comic strip. In order to give the reader of the present volume some idea of the magnitude of Hogarth's work, here is a brief chronology of Tarzan's adventures as they were imagined by Hogarth.

The dates given here are the dates of publication in the United States.

Tarzan in the City of Gold: May 9, 1937—when Hogarth first took over the episode in mid-course—to October 3, 1937.

Tarzan and the Boers: October 10, 1937 to May 29, 1938.

Tarzan and the Chinese: June 5 to November 20, 1938.

Tarzan and the Pygmies: November 27, 1938 to May 14, 1939.

Tarzan and the Amazons: May 21 to July 23, 1939.

First published drawings of "Tarzan" signed by Burne Hogarth, May 9, 1937.

Tarzan

by Edgar Rice Burroughs

VANISHING HOPE

OVER THE HEADS OF THE CROWD SAILED THE MIGHTY JUNGLE LORD, INTO THE WATERS OF THE DREAD LAGOON

ALREADY ONE OF THE MONSTROUS SPEARFISH WAS NEARING PRINCESS LEECIA.

"OH, WHY DIDN'T YOU RUN AWAY?" THE GIRL SHOUTED. "NOW, BOTH OF US ARE DOOMED!"

TARZAN DID NOT ANSWER. THE FULL FORCE OF HIS ENERGY WAS DEVOTED TO A DESPERATE EFFORT TO SAVE THE GIRL...

HE SAW THAT HE WAS TOO LATE TO JERK HER FROM THE PATH OF THE SPEEDING MONSTER.

BUT HIS HAND LEAPED OUT, CLUTCHED THE DEADLY SPIKE, AND SWERVED IT FROM ITS HUMAN TARGET.

THEN, STILL HOLDING TO THE SPEAR, HE WHIPPED OUT HIS KNIFE AND KILLED THE MONSTER.

MOLOCAR WAS ALARMED. HE MUST NOT LET TARZAN DO WHAT NO MAN HAD EVER DONE BEFORE—ESCAPE THE DEMON-FISH.

Copr. 1940, Edgar Rice Burroughs, Inc.—Tm. Reg. U.S. Pat. Off. Produced by Famous Books and Plays; Distributed by UNITED FEATURE SYNDICATE, Inc.

HE WHISPERED TO ONE OF THE LESSER PRIESTS, WHO HASTENED INTO THE TEMPLE ON HIS SECRET MISSION.

NOW TARZAN TOOK THE GIRL IN TOW, TRYING TO EVADE THE SEA-DEMONS.

BUT IT SEEMED A VAIN ATTEMPT, FOR HOW COULD HE REACH THE PLAZA WHICH WAS HIGH ABOVE THE LAGOON?

AND THE MONSTERS WERE CLOSING IN FAST, THEIR SPEARS FLASHING EAGERLY. NEXT WEEK: **INTO THE DEPTHS**

HOGARTH—

"Tarzan," July 7, 1940.

Tarzan and the Boers (2nd episode): July 30, 1939 to April 28, 1940.

Tarzan and the Peoples of the Sea and the Fire: May 5, 1940 to April 27, 1941.

Tarzan against Dagga Ramba: April 27, 1941 to April 26, 1942.

Tarzan and the Fatal Fountain: May 1 to August 2, 1942.

Tarzan and the Barbarians: August 9, 1942 to October 24, 1943.

Tarzan against Kandullah and the Nazis: October 31, 1943 to March 12, 1944.

Tarzan against Don Macabre: March 19 to July 30, 1944.

Tarzan against the Nazis: August 6, 1944 to March 11, 1945.

Tarzan against the Goru-Bongara Monster: March 18 to July 8, 1945.

Tarzan against Orizu Khan: Hogarth drew this episode from July 15 to November 25, 1945, when he temporarily withdrew from "Tarzan" to launch "Drago."

Tarzan on the Island of Ka-Gor: Hogarth took over this episode from August 10 to December 7, 1947.

Tarzan and N'Ani: December 14, 1947 to May 9, 1948.

Tarzan on the Island of Mua-Ao: May 16, 1948 to May 1, 1949.

Tarzan and the Ononoes: May 8 to October 23, 1949.

Tarzan and the Adventurers: October 30, 1949 to July 16, 1950.

Tarzan and the Wild Game Hunter: begun July 23, 1950 and abandoned by Hogarth August 20, 1950.

In 1945, unhappy with the conditions imposed upon him by United Feature Syndicate, Hogarth gave Robert Hall Syndicate an original creation, "Drago," which made its first appearance in November of the same year. The action of "Drago" takes place in Argentina, but we quickly come back to the universe dear to the author: tormented landscapes, sinister shadows, imposing silhouettes. Baroque imagination runs wild in the opulence of the women's costumes and in the phantasmagoric atmosphere, halfway between carnival and Grand Guignol, in which the strip is drenched. The story's hero, Drago, who is a more youthful Tarzan, and his comic sidekick Tabasco are up against the enterprises of the sinister Baron Zodiac, a Nazi whose only dream is revenge. The adventures are somewhat conventional, but the style makes up for the banality of the scenario. Never had Hogarth's talent risen to such expressionistic fury as with "Drago." Alas, this comic strip was to know but a brief existence. Late in 1946, it disappeared, leaving behind a feeling of frustration and regret for what the strip might have become.

The next year, yielding to the repeated solicitations of the United Feature Syndicate (UFS), Hogarth took over "Tarzan" again, but not before he had obtained more advantageous conditions, including the freedom to write his own scenarios. It was then that the style of "Tarzan" reached its highest peak of perfection and the hero was most intimately shaped by the vision of his author. Hogarth stated in a recent interview: "I wanted to give 'Tarzan' a sense of commitment toward the world. . . . I wanted to make Tarzan the primitive into a humane hero, to bring him from the state of nature to the state of intelligence." At the same time that he resumed "Tarzan," Hogarth created, still for UFS, his only humor strip, "Miracle Jones," in which a timorous character dreams his life, a little like Walter Mitty. The work, which marks for Hogarth a break in style, is curious and not without merit, but it met with little popular success and Hogarth regretfully abandoned it in November, 1947.

A new conflict was soon to arise between the author of "Tarzan" and UFS, this time about the foreign rights to "Tarzan." When his contract expired in 1950, Hogarth declined to renew it. He finally left "Tarzan" and the comic strip in order to devote his time to the School of Visual Arts which had sprung from a nucleus of people who had gone to Hogarth to receive his professional advice and guidance. It is, today, one of the most important and comprehensive centers of art training in the United States. The curriculum includes not only drawing and all the other art disciplines, but also photography, animated cartoon, and cinema. A whole new generation of cartoonists has come forth from the School of Visual Arts: Wallace Wood, Al Williamson, Dick Hodgins, Gil Kane, etc. Burne Hogarth assumed the functions there of Director of Curriculum, while at the same time he taught classes in drawing, anatomy, and art history. [*Editor's note: Hogarth retired from the School of Visual Arts in 1970 to devote himself fully to painting, drawing, and writing.*]

Ever since Hogarth left "Tarzan,"—a decision, he points out, which was "taken with no regret then, and contemplated with no regret now"—Hogarth has applied his efforts to etching and primarily to painting. His creations are all stamped with a highly personal style. He is also the author of two books, *Dynamic Anatomy* and *Drawing the Human Head*. [*Editor's note: Another book,* Dynamic Figure Drawing, *was published by Watson-Guptill in 1970.*] For Hogarth no lesson is ever lost: the teachings of the masters of classical art help him to solve the thorny methodological problems of the comic strip; in turn, the narrative techniques of the comics find their way, simplified and stripped to the essentials, into his etchings and his canvases.

In spite of the success of the "Tarzan" strip, appreciation of Hogarth's work has been long in coming. Art reviewers have ignored him. Even the historians of the comic strip hardly discussed him at all a short time ago. It took the labors of the Society of Study and Research in Pictorial Literatures to present his name to the general public. The 1966 exhibition of his works set up by *Socerlid* in the galleries of the French Society of Photography had lasting repercussions on both sides of the Atlantic. [*Editor's note: The Société d'Etudes et de Recherches de Littératures Dessinées (or Socerlid) was founded in November, 1964 at a Left Bank café in Paris by Pierre Couperie, Proto Destefanis, Edouard Francois, Claude Moliterni, and Maurice Horn.*]

In a profession where most artists are merely content to turn out an adequate (and sometimes less than adequate) product, Burne Hogarth stands, if not alone, at least in the company of very few peers. He has been dogged in his decision to stand by the tenets of his artistic calling and to go beyond mere craftsmanship by a conscious effort at something higher. He wanted to transcend the limitations of the medium of the comic strip as it was defined when he took over "Tarzan" in 1937, and force it into a new departure. Hesitant at first, Hogarth ventured forth in his bold experiments until he perfected his own unique drawing and narrative style.

This was by no means a simple achievement of technique. In Chapter 10 of *A History of the Comic Strip* by Pierre Couperie, Maurice Horn, et al., Claude Moliterni attempts a descriptive analysis of Hogarth's method, based on the observation of a single Sunday page of "Tarzan":

One of the most striking examples of accelerated narrative technique is to be found in a "Tarzan" page drawn by Burne Hogarth; the page demonstrates the author's preoccupations and leads to a type of composition that sacrifices plot to esthetics. Let us consider a specific case.

First scene: a panoramic view of Tarzan in profile, running.

Second scene: same plane, background shortened, character seen from behind. The lines of force . . . increase, and we feel an augmentation of internal tension.

Third scene: closer general view, the dramatic content of which indicates the hesitation of the surrounded Tarzan, who is searching for an escape.

Fourth scene: vertical view, in which Tarzan, surrounded, is about to make a supreme effort.

"Tarzan," October 10, 1948.

Tarzan

by EDGAR RICE BURROUGHS

TRAVELING SWIFTLY, TARZAN CAME AT LAST TO THE FOOT OF THE ASHANGOLA MOUNTAINS AND TO WHAT HE BELIEVED TO BE THE PASS DESCRIBED BY PHILIP RANSOME.

"THOSE BOULDERS ON THE EDGE OF THAT LEDGE," TARZAN MUSED, "WERE PLACED THERE BY HUMAN HANDS!"

"BLOOD-STAINS---AND A BROKEN SPEAR! RANSOME'S STORY MUST BE TRUE. I WONDER WHAT BECAME OF THE BODIES OF THE BEARERS?" HE MUSED.

A SUDDEN NOISE AND HE GLANCED UP QUICKLY---TO FIND HIMSELF IN THE PATH OF DESTRUCTION!

WITH THE SPEED AND AGILITY OF MANU THE MONKEY, HE LEAPED, HIS FINGERS AND TOES LOCATING SLIGHT PROJECTIONS IN THE SHEER WALL.

FROM HIS PRECARIOUS PERCH, TARZAN GAZED ACROSS THE NARROW GORGE. SEVERAL HUGE, ROUND, DARK OBJECTS ROLLED OUT OF SIGHT ALONG THE HIGH LEDGE.

HOGARTH

5/22

Copr. 1949 Edgar Rice Burroughs, Inc.—Tm. Reg. U.S. Pat. Off.
Distr. by United Feature Syndicate, Inc.

950

"Tarzan," May 22, 1949.

In a single drawing, Hogarth could have . . . summarized the scene in a long text, but by decomposing the action and opening up with a panoramic view (first scene), he created suspense and made the reader realize the bond between the antagonists (scenes 2 and 3). . . . The sudden appearance, in the foreground of the Negroes who surround Tarzan is a shock device and it achieves a high dramatic and kinetic tension.

With regard to the general layout of the pictures, Hogarth, until 1945, utilized the four-strip system created by Foster. That year saw the birth of Hogarth's own beloved brainchild, "Drago." This strip, with its silhouette-like characters on a white ground, elimination or interruption of the frame, silhouettes standing away from circles sometimes decorated in Japanese fashion, and varied types of frames, was an abortive attempt to break away from "Tarzan's" traditional frames. Upon resuming "Tarzan" in 1947, Hogarth adopted a new formula better suited to the dynamics of his style: three horizontal and three vertical strips. Over this grille, composed of nine equal rectangles, he ranged at ease, combining them in twos and threes, vertically, horizontally, or in four-block squares. He thus obtained a flexible, serene layout that accentuated his violently energetic style. . . . In the last forty-six pages of "Tarzan" Hogarth once again modified his layout by limiting himself to three vertical strips over two horizontals. His draftsmanship then achieved maximum expressiveness by the extensive use of panoramic views and very dramatic scenes.

Hogarth's main preoccupation was not to perfect a style suitable to his particular talents and tastes, but to solve the artistic problems of the comics. This constant search for new horizons sets Hogarth apart even from such talented colleagues as Alex Raymond and Harold Foster. Foster and Raymond, after having mastered their respective styles, were satisfied to apply their acquired skills to the problems at hand. Hogarth, on the other hand, constantly introduced new problems into his strip, problems against which he could pit his skills.

The reader who is fortunate enough to own or have access to the whole collection of the Hogarth "Tarzans" notices that, building up slowly, the successive pages do not seem to follow a geometric progression, but blend into one another. It is the total that dictates the necessary order of the parts. If Hogarth does not follow faithfully the letter of the narrative, it is because he is preoccupied with the spirit of the story. He aims for a visual treatment that has the grandeur of a myth (and the fact that "Tarzan" has assumed the proportions of a myth cannot be denied). He spurns the anecdotal in favor of the thematic, the literal for the symbolic.

Paul Spencer comments on the development of Hogarth's style in his article "Hogarth's Monsieur Tarzan," Evergreen, Colorado, ERBdom, No. 28, November, 1969:

It is the pictures that matter, anyway—and what pictures they are! Reproduced [in *Tarzan, Seigneur de la Jungle*] in far better color than one ever sees in a newspaper, they come across with staggering dramatic impact. Moreover, the power of Hogarth's work seems to have increased as time went on. There is a marked progression from "Boers" to "N'Ani" and then on through the other sequences to crescendo in "Tarzan and the Adventurers," the insipidity of whose plot is far more than offset by the explosive drama of the drawings. . . .

He [Hogarth] knows, too, that the central figure in his drawings cannot exist in a vacuum. All the elements in the foreground and background of each panel make up a unified and expressive composition. In combination with the obsessively painstaking workmanship, this produces panel after panel that could be hung on a wall, if not as fine art at least as a coherent, eloquent, and even handsome example of highly skilled graphics.

It is illuminating to examine the abundant body of critical writings about Hogarth's works, because the critics reveal how layer upon layer of meaning can be discovered in Hogarth's *oeuvre*. That such complexity exists in a "mere" cartoonist is proof both of the art of the comics and of the artistry of Hogarth. The French author and journalist Francis Lacassin wrote in his essay "Hogarth between Wonder and Madness," Paris, Giff-Wiff, No. 13, 1st Quarter 1965:

Hogarth's universe is unremittingly shaken by a frightful tempest which dislocates its angles and deforms its perspectives, at the same time that a brutal and frigid wind moves across it. Under the tempest's bite, the living creatures become agitated, vegetation bows down, and trees wring their branches in the hope of escaping the fury of a storm whose center is Tarzan's body. This is a body which the artist will strive to reproduce in every position, possible and impossible, abandoning the principles of a humdrum realism . . .

Only the cinema, because it is itself in motion, can bring to life the notions of volume and depth . . . . Thus Hogarth will make ample use of its technique and its language . . . a montage of images composed in accordance with cinematic techniques . . . he modifies his visual field and its orientation with close-up, cross-cutting, downward shot, upward shot, panning and the placement of certain characters or objects, thereby giving a variety of depth to his perspective.

For the integrating vision of Foster, who expresses himself by means of the scene rendered in its totality, like a single-shot sequence, Hogarth has substituted his own, more analytical vision, which endeavors to show not a succession of *tableaux*, but the same scene perceived from different angles. . . . In this manner demands of emphasis dictate the modifications of the narrative structure . . .

The twists of the plot are arranged to serve a set purpose: the dynamic depiction of Tarzan's anatomy. Pitted against him are opponents—men or beasts—well-suited to free his kinetic energy. It is clear that Hogarth does not strive so much to develop the point of the narrative as to express the inner drama of the action: the furor of the bodies often reflects the torment of the souls. Rather than tell the story word for word, he elects to represent some of its significant moments. Nearly always these correspond to phases of acute dramatic tension . . .

In turn, the atmosphere yields to the frenzy which consumes the living. Nature seems in a feverish trance: the grass and the trees bow under the threat of an ever-raging storm and fire stirs up the bowels of the earth and illuminates, in some apocalyptic explosion, the peaks of the volcanoes. Still waters try to conceal quicksands. Moving waters, rolling into foamy swells, meditate some frightful tidal wave. . . . A high wall is destined to bring into display the hero's muscles while he climbs over it; a branch stands out so he might crouch down in a simian position in order to jump on his enemies; a sugarloaf-shaped rock allows Tarzan to hug it with nonchalance and contemplate the horizon.

. . . Foster's brush gave Tarzan a simplicity of purpose. Hogarth's invisible camera makes him into an actor whose behavior is shaped by the needs of the *mise-en-scène*. Theatrical convention succeeds realistic simplicity. The secondary characters in their death throes, the monarchs in the affirmation of their tyranny, and Tarzan in his most familiar gestures strike up stage postures, charged and speeded-up by the artist's obsession with dynamic action. The well-known pose of a figure standing with his arms folded against the chest meant only undisturbed power to Foster. As seen by Hogarth, the pose breathes defiance. The gesture of the arm with pointed finger has now become both sententious and imperious. The somewhat quaint majesty with which Foster sometimes froze his [*Tarzan's*] silhouette is eclipsed by Hogarth's feverish contortions, signs of impatience, surprised starts, and interrupted motions of the figure.

The hero has changed his manners and the company he keeps. Tarzan is no longer the knight of the quiet mornings who, sliding down a vine, would leave nature's palace

Tarzan
by EDGAR RICE BURROUGHS

FOLLOWING A BATTLE WITH THE FANATICAL DAGOMBAS, TARZAN ESCAPED BY DIVING INTO THE LAKE. CHAKA, HOWEVER, REMAINED BEHIND AND SPIED THE APE-MAN AS HE CLIMBED FROM THE WATER.

INSTANTLY THE CHASE WAS ON. YELLING SAVAGELY, THE DAGOMBAS SWEPT ALONG THE BEACH. GRIMLY, TARZAN SPED DOWN THE LEDGE.

MOVING TOWARD THE BEACH, HE SAW CHAKA AND HIS WARRIORS RUSH TO INTERCEPT HIM.

SHOUTING TRIUMPHANTLY, THE DAGOMBAS CLOSED IN FROM TWO DIRECTIONS. HE, WHO HAD BROKEN THE STRICTEST TABOO OF THE SERPENT GOD, WAS TRAPPED!

HOGARTH.

4/9

996

TARZAN WHEELED TO AVOID THE TRAP. THEN, FROM THE OPPOSITE SIDE, ANOTHER GROUP CONVERGED.

"Tarzan," April 9, 1950.

The Magic of Burne Hogarth   15

to meet, in the world of man, benevolent kings on shaky thrones, languid princesses, foolhardy explorers, farmers blessed with venerable beards, and valiant, industrious wives. He has changed into an intransigent fighter for justice whose flexible body seems to ignore rest or even vertical position. Protecting the weak and defenseless, he moves across the jungle in a succession of leaps, in positions which range between the horizontal and the diagonal. When he darts down from a tree-top, it is in a brutal and vertical dive . . . . Waiting below are mad scientists, rich traders, beasts, slaves, ivory-pated high priests, or lascivious, imperious queens. Gone is the time when Tarzan used to bask in the sun, chat with his apes, or calmly saddle up his horse. If he is immobile at times, he sits in a crouching position with his body bent in half, as though tied in a knot, ready to jump. When he consents to rest, it is in the manner of those athletes who, between rounds, do not let their muscles relax, but flex them anew for a later effort. And when, sometimes, the artist, repressing the hero's impulses, freezes him in a kind of majesty, one feels underneath, as under the marble envelope of Michelangelo's *Moses*, a stirring of ill-concealed fervor mixed with impatience.

Six years later, in the light of new research, Lacassin again assesses the art and meaning of Hogarth's work in chapter 11 of his recently published book, *Tarzan or the Intense Knight*, Paris: Union Générale d'Editions, 1971:

> When, in 1937, he [*Hogarth*] is about to give Tarzan enduring qualities—which still assert themselves more than twenty years later—his knowledge of Burroughs' novels comes from his adolescent reading. But this knowledge does not extend beyond six or seven titles. He cites among others: *Tarzan of the Apes, Tarzan and the Ant-Men, Tarzan at the Earth's Core, Tarzan the Untamed, Tarzan the Terrible*. But Burroughs' universe is only a component of Hogarth's universe, a component in competition with Hogarth's other interests. Hogarth is fascinated by Oriental art, by the vehemence of Goya's work, by the suffering portrayed by Grünewald, by the vitality of Rubens' compositions, by the narrative technique of the cinema, by the classicism of Greek sculpture, and by the ideas of German expressionism. Hogarth is also interested in architecture and has a broad knowledge of anthropology . . .
>
> . . . Along with Milton Caniff, Alex Raymond, Hal Foster and Chester Gould, Hogarth is one of the masters of the modern strip. He remains a master, although he retired twenty years ago. Among them he is the only one to have had enduring influence, an influence extending to many different countries. Most of the work of adventure strip artists—especially those who have illustrated or drawn Tarzan—bears Hogarth's stamp. . . . Hogarth fascinates because he is one of the few comic strip artists to have thoughts on the comic strip, its technique, its artifices, its mission, and its destiny.

Pierre Couperie wrote at the end of a long article on the American comic strip entitled "Les Bandes dessinées américaines," in *Terre d'Images*, Paris, March 11, 1966:

> Burne Hogarth's books—his treatise on *Dynamic Anatomy*, in particular—his etchings and paintings . . . are all evidence of the fact that the comic strip is not necessarily the refuge of ignorant and plodding hacks. It can be an art thoroughly thought out by its authors. This fact irritates comic strip art's traditional enemies and some of its practitioners—those who are incapable of working up to such a high level.

If Hogarth's position in the field of comic strip art seems assured, what about his place in the rarified atmosphere of what is commonly referred to as the "fine arts"? Again, European critics have proved more responsive than their American counterparts. The Europeans have sensed all the markings of an original artist in Hogarth, despite the fact that they were aware only of a small portion of Hogarth's considerable *oeuvre*. When Hogarth's work was exhibited in Europe, the critics were almost unanimously favorable. Here are some of the reviews. To begin, I will quote a passage from Pierre Mazars in *Le Figaro Littéraire,* Paris, March 10, 1966. Mazars writes:

> There is a curious and delightful phenomenon at the gallery of the French Society of Photography, rue de Montalembert: comic strips are being exhibited. These strips are created by a master of this art form . . . Burne Hogarth. He is fifty-five years old, one of the founders of the School of Visual Arts in New York City—this school instructs hundreds of students—and the author of two treatises on anatomy and its application in painting.
>
> Hogarth's work is permeated with scholarship: his waves resemble those of the Oriental artists; his figures reveal a passion for Michelangelo; and the layouts of his scenes are derived from the great classical compositions, like *The Continence of Scipio.* Indeed, one can easily detect the application of the Golden Mean in his drawings. With Hogarth the comics become the last refuge of classicism, to the chagrin of the practitioners of Pop Art who appreciate the comics so much.

Eric Leguèbe writes in *Le Parisien Libéré,* Paris, February 22, 1966:

> Hogarth is chiefly known, and rightly so, as the illustrator of Tarzan's adventures. From 1937 to 1950, he has signed some 606 pages on this subject, but only 350 have been published in France. The most interesting aspect of the remarkable exhibition devoted to him by *Socerlid,* with the cooperation of the American Cultural Center in Paris, is the discovery of certain unknown aspects of the Tarzan myth under the pen of Hogarth. The study of Tarzan's character and its evolution is facilitated by the fact that some pictures are enlarged and there are numerous panels on which different versions of certain drawings are disposed. Some of the documents included in the exhibition explain the influence of Michelangelo, Bresdin, and Japanese prints upon Hogarth's graphic style. These influences are acknowledged by Hogarth himself.
>
> Hogarth, however, is not only the demiurge of Tarzan, but a co-founder of the School of Visual Arts in New York City, and the author of two treatises on human anatomy. Some of the original drawings for his treatises are now being exhibited at the Montalembert Gallery. This exhibition is painstaking and comprehensive and it includes some canvases by Hogarth. These canvases reveal him as a painter of the fantastic and of a universe that is both classical and fabulous.

Original 1946 title page as reprinted in *Drago* (Paris, Editions Serg, 1971).

Marc Albert-Levin in *Les Lettres Françaises,* Paris, February 24, 1966 writes about the exhibition at the galleries of the French Society of Photography, held with the collaboration of the American Cultural Center:

Hogarth infuses "Tarzan" with his entire artistic culture: his oft-stated admiration for Michelangelo and the great baroque painters, his affinities for German expressionism, his passion for the art of the Orient. . . . Photographically enlarged [*in the exhibition*] his drawings, the framing of which owes much to photography, reveal an incontestable academic mastery and an atmosphere which is at times reminiscent of Gustave Moreau or the work of the surrealists. The exhibition brings to light the conventions of the [*comic strip*] medium, which contribute to the mysterious power of these comics which have left a lasting mark on many a child's memory. It is incomparably superior to the "Booms" and "Whaaams" of the American Lichtenstein who, by an odd irony, in the same impersonal and cold mode, currently reproduces . . . abstract forms.

It is interesting to note that Burne Hogarth, who co-founded the School of Visual Arts in New York City, teaches drawing and anatomy in a curriculum which also includes cinema, photography, and comic art. He considers Pop Art "a dubious venture," but closely follows the progress of Op Art.

Jacques Michel writes in *Le Monde,* Paris, March 11, 1966:

The bandwagon is being hitched-up: comic art follows in the wake of narrative realism, now in fashion in the art world. Since the "pop artists" have taken to reproducing the contents of the comics as a part of what is popularly called reality, why shouldn't the original comics be worthy of consideration? Burne Hogarth, to whom an exhibition is paying homage, started as a comic strip artist; collectors are now buying his works as a painter. It seems that today's realism is yesterday's academicism. However, as a cartoonist, Hogarth deserves more than this and his work reveals numerous esthetic sources.

Cinema has influenced both the technique by which he frames each illustration, and the sequence in which he illustrates the narration. But at the core of Hogarth's style is the combination of text-image. . . . Tarzan, Burne Hogarth's central character, is seen within a space which is constantly changing. There are downward or upward shots, close-ups or long shots. The image is modified to serve the story, but the rhythm of images becomes more and more dynamic. Deprived of this tense and expressive "motion," the comic strip would disintegrate. This is where all Hogarth's artistry resides. The convolutions of Tarzan's athletic body, presented in anatomically descriptive panels, show in every muscle. The figure's poses are taken from the subject's of Michelangelo and Leonardo Da Vinci. It is indeed in the work of these great artists, and in the work of Rembrandt, Goya, Brueghel . . . that Hogarth finds his models and not in life. However, the over-all execution clearly reveals other influences as well—expressionism, baroque dynamism, and surrealism.

The whole action—forest, objects, animals, musculature—is drawn with an exacerbated line in order to give more intensity to the strip's total emotional impact. Tarzan is a cocktail of the eternal trilogy of the American cinema: 'thrills, sex, and blood.'

Gerald Gassiot-Talabot in *Les Annales,* Paris, April, 1966 writes:

A careful study of the very skillful composition and the imaginative freedom which characterize Hogarth's work, reveals that his comic pages, influenced by baroque painting, have a conception of stunning power. In the multiple situations in which he must place his character, Hogarth never yields to redundancy. He endows the adventures of the Ape-Man with a sense of wonder, all the more apparent because of the photographic enlargement of his pictures [*in the exhibition*].

Hogarth . . . is today at the head of a very important art school in New York City and has specialized in anatomical studies. The reason for this predilection can be understood when one sees the anatomical forms of his hero who is at the center of his three-

MULTIPLE-ACTION STUDY from *Dynamic Figure Drawing* (Watson-Guptill Publications, 1970).

dimensional compositions. The artist's conception is very classical, by necessity; yet, it is saved from academicism by the dynamic power of motion, a kind of fury which runs through the action. Hogarth yields to a visual delirium when he depicts the depths of a river teeming with wild beasts, or the grandiose skyline of an imaginary city. In the necessary haste of his work, in the whirlwind which engulfs his characters, Hogarth does not have the time to indulge in the smugness upon which academic art feeds.

Although the narrative, in itself, conforms to certain standards and certain conventions necessitated by the comic strip form, the drawing allows unlimited freedom, and Hogarth's fertile mind does not hesitate to take full advantage of it.

These writings and others—published in Europe and Latin America—have established Burne Hogarth as an artist of stature abroad. The American art establishment has been slower to appreciate comic art in general, and Hogarth's art in particular. However, some critics and academics have recently become aware of what has been happening: Hogarth was among the featured artists in the 1971 exhibition of comic strips at the University of Maryland. In the catalogue of the exhibition, Hogarth's work was summarized thus:

In 1950, Hogarth quit the strip to found the New York School of Visual Arts. The impact of his work on subsequent realistic strips was considerable, but the scope of the adventures he created, as well as his technical accomplishment in rendering them, remains unequaled; his followers never quite realized the dramatic agitation that pervades his "Tarzan."

THE MINOTAUR, 1968. 24 x 18¾, black ink on white paper.

In the August 30, 1971 issue of *The Nation,* no less an art critic than Lawrence Alloway wrote:

> The individuation of comic artists must include reference to Burne Hogarth who, when he took over the "Tarzan" strip, brought to it a sophisticated sense of mannerism (Tarzan as a post-Michelangelesque male) and of Japanese art (in the flat patterning of jungle flora).

Finally, the "75 Years of the Comics" exhibition, held at the New York Cultural Center in 1971, gave Burne Hogarth the full recognition that he deserved and which had been so long in coming.

Burne Hogarth is now widely recognized as the greatest living artist of the comics. This fact can readily be attested by the flood of critical notices and reportorial articles that follow each of the exhibitions in which he is a participant, and each of his appearances at one of the many conventions of comic strip artists and critics, now regularly taking place throughout the world. Hogarth's fame has mushroomed spectacularly in the last decade, as amateurs and professionals discover the astonishing range of his work. However, Hogarth's sense of humor and his natural earthiness have prevented him from playing the part of the celebrity. But a celebrity he has become, and, as such, he is always good copy for an article or an interview. Further, a tract on the comics would not be complete now without some admiring mention of Hogarth's work.

In the United States, where the comics have not been regarded as a serious art form until very recently, the adulation which Burne Hogarth receives might seem astonishing. Predictably, Hogarth's artistry was recognized first in France and has been proclaimed loudest in that country. However, the admiration of the French for Hogarth is shared with no less enthusiasm (and scholarship) by the Latin-Americans. Here, for example, is what the Argentinian weekly *Primera Plana* had to say in a lengthy article devoted to Hogarth in their October 15, 1968 issue:

> Only the United States could afford the luxury of producing this kind of playboy of the arts, a noble mixture of Walt Disney and an Oxford don, sprinkled with the sportsmanlike nonchalance of a Joe DiMaggio. . . . Hogarth . . . is an anthropocentric humanist for whom man is the measure of all things. He is no doubt aware of this since he describes the Renaissance with ill-concealed nostalgia: "In that epoch, the artist was the fountain of all things. Now, in contrast, and there is no doubt about it, the scientists have killed us."

Another enlightened Argentinian weekly, *Gente,* in an article by Victor Sueiro, chose to give a different view of Hogarth's multi-faceted personality. In an article titled "Tarzan's Daddy," Buenos Aires, *Gente,* October 16, 1968, Sueiro writes:

> The draughtsman of "Tarzan," the man who used his pencil to delineate the muscular figure of the athlete of the jungle, is now in Buenos Aires attending the Biennial of the Comics in the Instituto Torcuato di Tella.
>
> He is a bit on the portly side, fifty-six years old, talks almost non-stop, is named Burne Hogarth, and doesn't smoke, a habit he may have picked up from the character he drew for thirty years. . . . [*Editor's note: Hogarth actually drew Tarzan for thirteen years.*]

[*Sueiro*] What did you read when you were a child?

[*Hogarth*] As far as books are concerned, I read a lot of Jack London, Fenimore Cooper, Robert Louis Stevenson, Charles Dickens. . . . I did not read any comic strips at that time. Some years later stories and tales with Victorian illustrations were published. They delighted me. I remember *Alice in Wonderland* very well. It was illustrated by Tenniel.

[*Sueiro*] What about the first comic you ever read in your life?

[*Hogarth*] The first one was called "The Brownies." . . . The story was full of action, and involved such things as good and bad gnomes, enchanted castles. It was a delight. Later the same feature inspired "The Teenie Weenies." . . . In fact, I don't know whether it is good or bad for me to reminisce about all this. I feel a delightful sensation and at the same time I feel a little old.

[*Sueiro*] Not as much as when you recall how you started doing "Tarzan," right?

[*Hogarth*] . . . I don't know, really. But getting back to "Tarzan" . . . I was telling you that the success of "Tarzan" owed much to the time when it was first drawn. This was a little after the start of the great depression: big corporations were crashing and misery was widespread. You will note that Tarzan is a man who makes his first appearance in the middle of the jungle; in some ways the jungle was not unlike the surroundings of everyone who happened to live in the United States of 1934. Tarzan finds himself—again, like the American people—without weapons to fight off all the perils. All he has is a small knife. . . . It is in this way, weaponless, naked, lost in the jungle with the desire to win by his own resources, that he most resembled the man in the street. People identified with him, not being aware in most cases of what Tarzan symbolized, and Tarzan was an enormous success.

[*Sueiro*] Do all comics reflect what is happening in real life at that time?

[*Hogarth*] Not always, but this has been the case with "Tarzan" and "Superman." "Superman" is another good example. "Superman" started as a comic strip in 1939, at a time which saw the definitive triumph of Hitler's ideas in Germany. Hitler *styled* himself precisely a "superman." . . . It is likely that the strip was also influenced by the writings of Nietzsche, who also advocated the superman, although in a different sense.

[*Sueiro*] Does this mean that the reader sees in the characters of the comic strip a reflection of his own, often unconscious, desires?

[*Hogarth*] Certainly. That also accounts for the success of James Bond movies. Bond is human but he has everything that today's mass-man yearns to possess: women, an exciting life, money, powerful automobiles, travel, good health, intelligence and—as if all this weren't enough—a special license to kill whoever he wants to. . . .

[*Sueiro*] Don't you think that there are many people who are ashamed to admit that they read comics?

[*Hogarth*] I suppose so. Usually, they are members of my own generation. Young people aren't ashamed to admit that they enjoy comic strips or comic books. One of my good friends is twenty-seven and he has been following the comics since childhood. We became friends because he wanted to meet the man who had been drawing his favorite character, and he came to see me one day. Today, being much younger than I, he still reads adventure strips. However, he is now professor of general philosophy and Greek at Boston University. There are many like him.

My generation looked down with contempt upon the comics because they reflected, to a great extent, the social conditions of their times. This was particularly upsetting to the middle class. Outcault, for instance, drew a feature which took place in the slums. The middle classes looked down their noses at it. . . . "Black Berries" was never accepted because it dealt with tales of the black people. . . . "Mutt and Jeff" was also harshly criticized because it was said that the strip glamorized the irresponsible life of racetrack bums. This explains why the people who enjoyed the comics would blush if they were caught reading them. . . . For the sophisticates of the time, it was like owning a lower-class passport. . . .

In an article entitled "Silence: Hogarth Speaks" in the Brazilian daily *O Estado do Sao Paulo, Sao Paulo,* November 25, 1970, José Moneres reports on a lecture given by Burne Hogarth:

The auditorium of the Museum of Art falls silent when Enrique Lipscyc asks if anyone has any questions to ask Hogarth about his lecture. Hogarth smiles and rises from behind the lectern. At that moment, thunderous applause rings out.

The public is showing its appreciation for the masterly lecture which revealed a different Hogarth to them. The creator of the best "Tarzan" pages has just proved that he is more than an exceptional draughtsman.

The Hogarth of today is a man of our times, deeply aware of the implications of his chosen medium. . . . Hogarth defined the comics as a . . . "complex device for transforming ideas into art. . . ." He then went on to compare comics with the cinema, stating that "a work of art . . . is more than a representation of reality; it has an additional symbolic meaning. . . ." "They [*the comics*] convey symbols of states of mind . . . tension, stress, apathy, sincerity. . . . You can read them easily, painlessly, and you can effortlessly perceive any minor variation in the expressions of the characters."

Many more articles, written in the same reverent tone, have appeared in Spain, the Netherlands, and even Germany and England, probably the two European countries most backward (until recently) in their appreciation of the comic strip.

Hogarth's fame abroad needs no further elaboration, but what about the United States? It is in the pages of little magazines put out by amateurs, "fanzines" as they have come to be called, that Hogarth's talent was first recognized in this country. Here is an assessment of Hogarth as an artist, made by Harry E. Habblitz, one of these "fans," in *Heroes Illustrated*, No. 2, Spring 1961:

HORSES, 1967. 11 x 8½, blue ballpoint pen on white paper.

HEAD OF AN OLD MAN, 1969. 14 x 8½, blue ballpoint pen on white paper.

However no criticism can negate Hogarth's very evident skill in the field of comic art. He offered the Sunday readers a fierce, grim-visaged, implacable demi-god, a jungle superman well designed to shock and thus interest a public inured through oversaturation of the printed image.

It might be significant to note that Hogarth's Tarzan flourished in the 1940's, a generation in which America was engaged in a grim kill or be killed struggle for survival. The naivety of the '20's which accepted Rex Maxon's Tarzan and the poverty of the '30's which enjoyed Foster's Tarzan had disappeared and the war years seemed to demand a Spartan-like no-nonsense hero of the right. The Sunday page was a weekly shot in the arm, a symbol of the reality of danger in life and an optimistic assurance that it could be surmounted with courage and action. Hogarth's Tarzan was as immediate and compelling as a tabloid headline—you might not always approve, but try and ignore it . . . impossible.

It should be noted that no subsequent Tarzan artist save Jessie Marsh (an obvious disciple of the Caniff style) has escaped the visual influence of the Hogarth style. John Celardo, the current artist; Rubimor and Bob Lubbers [*other artists who have drawn "Tarzan"*], who filled in between, were actually hampered by Hogarth's influence and unable to express their own personal concepts. Even today traces of Hogarth can be found in the Russ Manning comic book conception. Truly, as long as there is a Tarzan comic, there will always be a touch of the immortal Hogarth in the image.

Habblitz and a few others were voices in the wilderness, however. Universally recognized as a master, Burne Hogarth, at that time, remained an artist without honor in his own country. Declining to belong to a clique, preferring integrity to the hucksterism displayed by many of his colleagues, refusing to pander to commercial interests, Hogarth was never popular in the ranks of the cartooning profession. To those associations busily engaged in merchandising the comics under deceptive advertising, a man like Hogarth—who insisted that comics should be judged according to artistic standards and that cartoonists should be judged on their own merits—was a thorn in the side. They tried to keep him down or out. Even some of Hogarth's former students, turned cartoonists, begrudged him his rightful place. They resented the fact that they could never hope to equal their master. Therefore, it is not surprising that a book like Stephen Becker's *Comic Art in America* (commissioned by the Newspaper Comics Council in 1959) scarcely contains a reference to Hogarth, the better to extol the virtues of untalented, but safe, syndicate hacks.

As the cultural backwash from Europe and Latin America reaches our shores, a rediscovery of Hogarth is beginning to take place. As mentioned previously, the New York Cultural Center singled him out—along with Winsor McCay and George Herriman—for his "excellence of conception and execution." I have pointed out that Hogarth's work also constituted an important part of an exhibition of comic strips at the University of Maryland this year. The illustrations for this book alone prove that Hogarth is irreplaceable and, indeed, incomparable.

Hogarth had never before illustrated any of the original Edgar Rice Burroughs novels, except for a few months in 1947, when he penciled the "Tarzan" daily strip adapted from *Tarzan at the Earth's Core*. Since the present book is a transposition of Burroughs' first, and most famous, Tarzan novel, it is legitimate to inquire how Hogarth conceived the character of Tarzan, and how his characterization compares to that of Burroughs, and to that of the man who was the first to portray Tarzan in comic strip form, Harold Foster. Francis Lacassin tries to give an answer in "Hogarth between Wonder and Madness," Giff-Wiff, No. 13, 1st Quarter 1965:

In different ways, the two most famous Tarzan artists have succeeded in placing their hero within the great tradition of the marvelous which goes from the Bible and Homer to Fantômas and the manifestations of surrealism. Foster delimited his background first. He worked within the framework of daily reality to which he successfully gave a lightly fabulous coloration. Foster created a character who was inspired by the epic ideals of chivalry, warrior-poets, and love courts, and endowed him with a romantic fate. Having placed Tarzan at the heart of this reality, he then embalmed him in his own legend.

By contrast, the center of Hogarth's *oeuvre* is the fascination exercised by the living body, in this instance Tarzan's. Because Hogarth wished to see Tarzan moving and living in a manner beyond that which reality allows, he was forced to construct an imaginary universe around him which, in time, became deliberately fantastic. But the fantastic quality owes little to the intervention of the supernatural; more appropriately, it springs from a transformation of reality and from a violent depiction of feelings and values. In this world, stricken with unreality, Tarzan appears as an overwhelmingly realistic hero, stooping under the weight of the human condition.

Harry Habblitz [*op. cit.*] is even more forceful in his evaluation of Hogarth's Tarzan as a figure of myth:

Burne Hogarth, illustrator and sometime author of the Sunday Tarzan comic strip, was an acknowledged master of the genre. He created the most forceful image of a hero ever to battle through the comic pages.

He began as a successor to Hal Foster. However, he was not content to emulate the dean of comic illustrators. He fused illustration and cartooning together with a stylized strip that was and is unique. Hogarth realized that an adventure strip must stress action and drama above all else. He was also aware that a comic page is swiftly read and as swiftly discarded. Its very nature prohibits a leisurely perusal of subtle details. Hogarth's Tarzan was the result of his frank acceptance that a cartoon is that first, and not just an illustration. A wealth of accurate, realistic detail would only distract the reader from direct communication. He realized that Tarzan was a dream hero; not an ordinary man in the romantic past like "Val" of Ultima Thule. To draw Tarzan as a real man was out of the question; to fashion him as a demi-god, a grim, larger than life Hercules striding purposefully through everyman's conception of a mythical African jungle—this is the stuff of legends and Hogarth had the sense to realize it and the ability and courage to draw it as he saw it.

. . . In addition, Hogarth extended his incomparable talent for [*the depiction of*] human anatomy to his drawing of animals. He de-emphasized and sometimes disregarded their shaggy pelts, the better to stress muscle structure and action. Thus the animals were no longer creatures of instinct but became almost human in their single minded lust to kill. If Tarzan was the embodiment of the masculine dream to be as tall and irresistibly handsome as a Greek god with the strength of Hercules, then the animal kingdom became the symbol of evil incarnate.

More than any other artist—more, even, than most moviemakers—Hogarth established *his* Tarzan as the visual embodiment of the Lord of the Jungle. There is no doubt that many people genuinely believe Hogarth to be the creator of the famous character. In Europe and in South America, he has been widely hailed as "the father of Tarzan." In fact, this had happened so often that the Parisian weekly *Le Nouveau Candide,* December 26, 1967, felt called upon to issue a disclaimer:

No, the American Burne Hogarth, who has just spent a few days in Paris recently, is not, as he has been a bit too hastily called, the creator of "Tarzan." The real "inventor" of the athlete of the jungle still remains the novelist Edgar Rice Burroughs who, in 1914, made him the hero of one of his books. . . .

Hogarth's secret lies in the fact that his Tarzan is a re-creation rather than an interpretation. In this respect, Burne Hogarth ranks above Harold Foster, to whom his detractors never tire of comparing him.

Hogarth himself went to great lengths to explain his own conception of the character and the relevance of the character to him in "How I Imagine Tarzan," a chapter in *Tarzan, Seigneur de la Jungle* (Paris: Azur, 1967):

> To begin with, let me assert that the person we speak of as Tarzan is, in a way, not a person at all. He is in a real sense the antithesis of the figures in literature and romantic fiction who are called "individuals" . . . he is no one man, but *man* himself.
>
> As the central figure of a world-renowned comic strip, Tarzan, of course, is its hero. Now, the term "hero," in the idiomatic popular sense, can be assigned by simple association to any number of comic figures from Popeye to Bugs Bunny to L'il Abner. . . . These characters, and many others, are freely called "heroes"; however, when we use the term in this random manner and apply it to personalities who are boobs, louts, and clowns, who are fumblers and bunglers—characters who are pitiful and contemptible —we are touching the sleeve of the absurd. We are lifting up the pariah and the outcast and equating them with the hero; by this inverse process we insidiously create the anti-hero. . . .
>
> Tarzan, to be understood clearly, must stand singularly free from all such equivocal definitions. The figure Tarzan is unimpeachably an authentic hero. He is the epic man. . . . He is a modern archetype of that class of more-than-ordinary, universally recognized beings who leap to magical life in daydreams; he is the ideal hero, the sublime champion, the emancipated other side of ourselves, released from the oppressive prison of our routine existence. He is that nostalgic part of every one of us, born of ourselves and of our image, invincible and deathless . . . he is the incarnation of our secret desire to be

THE BULL, 1968. 14 x 16¾, brown and black Conté crayon on white paper.

free from every form of insignificance, frustration, and degradation. He is our own alter ego, our liberated second self of concentrated power, grandeur, and magnificence.

To me, Tarzan represents the best of men everywhere. His aspirations are of the highest because there are no base motives in him. In his world, there are no greater or lesser persons, no higher or lower peoples. Before him all men are equal. Nor does he merely believe in equality; he believes in acts that are virtuous and humane. . . .

In another sense, Tarzan is a symbol of equality in that he rejects the role of the victim and resists the status of the oppressed. In his dangerous environment, he is able to bring his great physical and mental powers to bear against the unreason of the brute world of nature and the brute nature of man, and with a fierce effort against supreme odds, to triumph.

As he will not be a victim, a servant or a slave, neither does he desire to be a master. Although he is "the Lord of the Jungle," he is no lord. . . . If Tarzan is a man of the elite, we must understand that his superiority does not come from rank or riches but from freedom. . . . His ethos is based on the innate free estate of all men. He seeks neither power nor control of the subservient. His desire is for autonomy rather than coercion, self-control rather than imposed discipline. His "lordship" is therefore no *over*-lordship.

He is always the exponent of justice, the even-handed dispenser of wisdom, the impartial guardian of fair play. He is the antithesis of vainglory, and self-conceit. . . . Without pretension he is generous—and gains in the giving when he has nothing whatever to gain for himself. . . .

There is something about Tarzan that is archaic and venerable. He is capable of inspiring an extraordinary feeling of respect and of generating an enormous aura of dignity. He has a charismatic personality which one associates with visionary leaders, prophets, and messiahs. His presence commands instant courtesy and radiates authority. . . . He can be lofty and remote; yet he is not aloof or unapproachable. While he can be unswervingly staunch and firm on matters of principle, he is warm and compassionate about matters of immediate need.

In spite of all these exalted qualities, Tarzan is nevertheless human. He is not above pleasure, nor beyond pain, and is certainly not free from misjudgment and error. He is not invulnerable; he is capable of suffering; he can be reduced to affliction and grief. . . . *He is no superman.* He has no arsenal of thunderbolts, cabalistic charms, or supersonic missiles. His only practical weapon of defense is the age-old, primitive device, the *long-tooth*, the knife of the dawn man in the morning of time. His weapon of attack is the same as that of any man, his intelligence; he survives, in a brutish world, by stratagems of test and trial. Hence, his passion is never irrelevant and his energies are always directed to a purpose; if he is capable of suffering, pain has a purpose and is never an end in itself. For this reason, his battles are never fanatic and he never becomes intoxicated with acts of martyrdom. In his adventures, he is never rash or extravagant. . . . He is born of trial and danger, but, wherever he goes, he brings reassurance and peace. He is energy, grace, and virtue. . . . He symbolizes the inevitable life source, the earth, the seed, the rain, the harvest, achievement, the triumph over adversity and death. . . .

He is a being who comes from an earlier time, sweeps comet-like through our lives toward another world, and leaves something unfinished, unspoken, unquiescent. He surges up from the myth-making substrata of childhood yearning, leaps into vigorous life, an elemental creature of fantasy, then flees in mirrored remembrance, a shimmering figment of myth and dream.

These words were written in 1967, but there could be no more fitting preface to the present volume. Burne Hogarth may have grown older since the moment, in 1937, when he first imagined Tarzan, but in his art, as in the mythological figure of the Lord of the Jungle, we will always find the luminous manifestation of everlasting youth.

There already exists a considerable volume of writings on the works, the career, and the art of Burne Hogarth. To make this bibliography manageable, only the most comprehensive, enlightening, or significant of them have been mentioned.

BOOKS

The following are books in which the work of Burne Hogarth is seriously studied and commented upon. Books that give only passing reference to Hogarth are omitted.

Blanchard, Gérard, *La Bande dessinée,* Verviers: Gérard, Collection "Marabout-Université," 1969.

Caen, Michel, with Jacques Lob and Jacques Sternberg, *Les Chefs d'oeuvre de la bande dessinée,* Paris: Planète, 1967.

Couperie, Pierre, Maurice Horn, et al., *A History of the Comic Strip,* New York: Crown, 1968.

(Collective), Catalogue of exhibition, *Burne Hogarth,* Paris: Socerlid, 1965.

Davidson, Sol, *Culture and the Comic Strip,* New York: New York University, Ph.D. Thesis, 1959.

Della Corte, Carlo, *I Fumetti,* Milan: Mondadori, 1961.

Hogarth, Burne, *Tarzan Jungle Lord,* Evergreen, Colorado: Opar Press, 1968. Essay: "How I Imagine Tarzan."

Horn, Maurice, *75 Years of the Comics,* Boston: Boston Book and Art and the New York Cultural Center, 1971.

—— *Tarzan, Seigneur de la Jungle,* Paris: Azur, 1967. Introduction.

Lipscyc, Enrique, *La Historieta Mundial,* Buenos Aires: Editorial Lipscyc, 1958.

Lacassin, Francis, *Tarzan, ou le Chevalier Crispé,* Paris: Union Générale d'Editions, 1971. Chapter XI.

O'Sullivan, Judith, *The Art of the Comic Strip,* College Park, Maryland: University of Maryland, 1971.

Strazzula, Gaetano, *I Fumetti,* Florence: Sansoni, 1970.

ARTICLES AND PAMPHLETS

The following writings deal with some important aspects of Hogarth's work.

(Anonymous), "Conversiones del ilustre Tarzan," *Analisis,* Buenos Aires, October 16, 1968.

(Anonymous), "O Homem que Desenhao O homem-Macaco," *O Estado de Sao Paulo,* Sao Paulo, October 16, 1968.

(Anonymous), "Plastica: La Visita del Padre de Tarzan," *Primera Plana,* Buenos Aires, October 15, 1968.

Albert-Levin, Marc, "Burne Hogarth," *Les Lettres Françaises*, Paris, February 24, 1966.

Bernazalli, Nino, "Tarzan," *Comics World*, Genoa, No. 3, June, 1968.

Bertieri, Claudio, "Tarzan ha 40 Anni," Genoa, *Il Lavoro*, April 19, 1968.

Caen, Michel, "Tarzan, beaucoup trop beau pour être honnète," *Giff-Wiff*, Paris, No. 13, 1st Quarter 1965.

Castelli, Alfredo, "Tarzan a Fumetti nei Quotidiani," *Comics Club*, Milan, No. 1, April-May, 1967.

Couperie, Pierre, "Les Bandes dessinées américaines. III: Burne Hogarth," Paris, *Terre d'Images*, March 11, 1966.

Della Corte, Carlo, "Il Fratellino de Tarzan," *Eureka*, Milan, August, 1968.

Gasca, Luis, "Tarzan," *El Correo Español*, Bilbao, April 14, 1968.

Gassiot-Talabot, Gérald, "De çà, de là," *Les Annales*, Paris, April, 1966.

Habblitz, Harry E., "Hogarth," *Heroes Illustrated*, Los Angeles, No. 2, Spring, 1969.

Hegerfors, Sture, "Tarzans Historia," *Kvallsposten*, Malmö, November 20, 1967.

Hogarth, Burne, "About those Comics," *Design*, Columbus, Ohio, January, 1950.

—— "Mes rapports avec Tarzan," *Giff-Wiff*, Paris, No. 13, 1st Quarter 1965.

Hume, David, "Michelangelo Set Trend for Tarzan," *Buenos Aires Herald*, Buenos Aires, October 11, 1968.

Lacassin, Francis, "Hogarth entre le Merveilleux et la Démence," Paris, *Giff-Wiff*, No. 13, 1st Quarter 1965.

—— "Introducing Hogarth," *Ibid*.

—— "L'Influence de Hogarth sur le dessin français," *Ibid*. (with Stève Parisot).

Leguèbe, Eric, "Burne Hogarth," *Phénix*, Paris, No. 7, 3rd Quarter 1968.

—— "Le Père de Tarzan expose à Paris," *Le Parisien Libéré*, Paris, February 22, 1966.

Michel, Jacques, "Tarzan ou le Mythe perdu," *Le Monde*, Paris, March 11, 1966.

Moneres, José, "Silencio: Hogarth Esta Falando," *O Estado de Sao Paulo*, Sao Paulo, November 25, 1970.

Parisot, Stève, "Tarzan, gestes et plastique," *Giff-Wiff*, Paris, No. 13, 1st Quarter 1965.

Spencer, Paul, "Hogarth's Monsieur Tarzan," *ERBdom*, Evergreen, Colorado, No. 28, November, 1969.

Strinati, Pierre, "Les Animaux vus par Tarzan," *Giff-Wiff*, Paris, No. 13, 1st Quarter 1965.

Sueiro, Victor, "El Papa de Tarzan," *Gente*, Buenos Aires, October 16, 1968.

Vielle, Henri, "Un cousin de Tarzan, Drago," *Giff-Wiff*, Paris, No. 13, 1st Quarter 1965.

Traini, Rinaldo, "Tarzan: il Mito della Liberta," *Sgt. Kirk*, Genoa, No. 6, December, 1967.

Zanotto, Piero, "Arriva Tarzan," *Nazione Sera*, Florence, July 11, 1967.

SELECTED MUSEOGRAPHY OF BURNE HOGARTH

1965   "10 Millions d'Images," Société Française de Photographie, Paris.

1966   "Burne Hogarth" (one-man show), Société Française de Photographie, Paris.

1966   "10 Millioni di Immagini," Museo Nazionale del Cinema, Turin.

1967   "Bande dessinée et Figuration narrative," Musée des Arts Décoratifs (Louvre), Paris.

1967   "Science-Fiction," Kunsthalle, Berne.

1967–68 "Science-Fiction," Musée des Arts Décoratifs (Louvre), Paris.

1968   "Exposition des Bandes dessinées," Palais des Beaux-Arts, Brussels.

1968   4th Salone Internazionale Dei Comics, Bastione San Regolo, Lucca.

1968   "La Bienal Mundial de la Historieta," Instituto Torcuato di Tella, Buenos Aires.

1968–69 "Panorama de la Bande dessinée," Maison de la Culture de Nevers, Nevers.

1969   "Le Monde de la Bande dessinée," Musées Royaux d'Art et d'Histoire, Brussels.

1969   "Burne Hogarth" (one-man show), Escola Panamericana de Arte, Sao Paulo.

1969   5th Salone Internazionale Dei Comics, Teatro del Giglio, Lucca.

1969   "Comic Strip," America House, Munich.

1969   Exhibition-Group Show, Lausanne.

1969–70 "Comic Strip," Akademie der Kunst, Berlin.

1970   6th Salone Internazionale Dei Comics, Lucca.

1970   "Exposicao De Quadrinhos," Museu de Arte, Sao Paulo.

1971   "The Art of the Comic Strip," University of Maryland Art Gallery, College Park, Maryland.

1971   "Strip 71," Nederlands Persmuseum, Amsterdam.

1971   "75 Years of the Comics," New York Cultural Center, New York.

EDGAR RICE BURROUGHS

1875–1950

From the day he was born on September 1, 1875, in Chicago, until he submitted his first story to *All-Story Magazine* in 1911, Edgar Rice Burroughs (ERB) failed in nearly everything he tried. He attended half a dozen public and private schools before he graduated from Michigan Military Academy. Unable to secure a commission in any military unit—including the Chinese Army—he finally enlisted in the Seventh U.S. Cavalry. But at the time of his discharge, he was still a private. A succession of 18 different jobs and business ventures followed his marriage in 1900 to Emma Centennia Hulbert, and by 1911 he was pawning his watch to buy food for his family.

Having doodled and sketched and written poetry for amusement most of his life, ERB decided at this low point in his career to see if the public would be as receptive to his imaginative ideas as were his friends and family. His first story, written on the back of old letterhead stationery from bankrupt businesses, brought him $400. Today, that story, "A Princess of Mars," is acclaimed as a turning point of twentieth-century science fiction.

Next, ERB wrote an historical novel. It was rejected. Penniless once again, he nearly quit. But a one-line letter from his publishers kept him going: "For Mike's sake, don't give up!" The next story would decide his future. It was *Tarzan of the Apes.*

Tarzan of the Apes was an astonishing success upon its appearance in *All-Story Magazine* in 1912, but it brought ERB a mere $700. And, since the story had originally appeared in a mere pulp magazine, it was rejected by practically every major book publisher in the country. However, when *Tarzan of the Apes* was finally printed in book form by A. C. McClurg & Company, it became 1914's best seller.

A torrent of novels followed: stories about the planet Venus, stories about the Apaches, Westerns, social commentaries, detective stories, and tales of the Moon and of the middle of the Earth. There were more and more Tarzan books. Ultimately, nearly 100 books bore ERB's name.

In 1918, Tarzan came to the screen. *Tarzan of the Apes,* starring Elmo Lincoln, was the first film in history to gross over a million dollars. Since then, 39 Tarzan films have been produced, each of them a great financial success. Although he liked to joke about them, ERB was bitterly disappointed with the Tarzan pictures. Often, he would not even go to see them. His Tarzan was a supremely intelligent, sensitive, truly civilized man: heroic, beautiful and, above all, free. The world knows well the semi-literate caricature Hollywood made of Tarzan.

By 1919, with financial security assured, ERB purchased the 550 acre estate of General Harrison Gray Otis in California, renaming it "Tarzana Ranch." Here, he wrote prodigiously and managed the worldwide enterprise that is now Edgar Rice Burroughs, Inc. In 1941, he volunteered to become a war correspondent and he finally returned home —as America's oldest correspondent—from the South Pacific only after suffering a series of heart attacks. He spent his remaining years as a semi-invalid in a modest house on Zelzah Avenue in Encino, California, where he set down his pen for the last time on March 19, 1950. His ashes were carried home to Tarzana, where, according to his own wish, they repose in an unmarked grave.

Burroughs scholar Henry Hardy Heins suggests that the last line of ERB's last Tarzan novel could be taken as the author's own unintentional valedictory: "Thank God for everything."

ROBERT M. HODES
Tarzana, California

BOOK ONE

OF THE APES

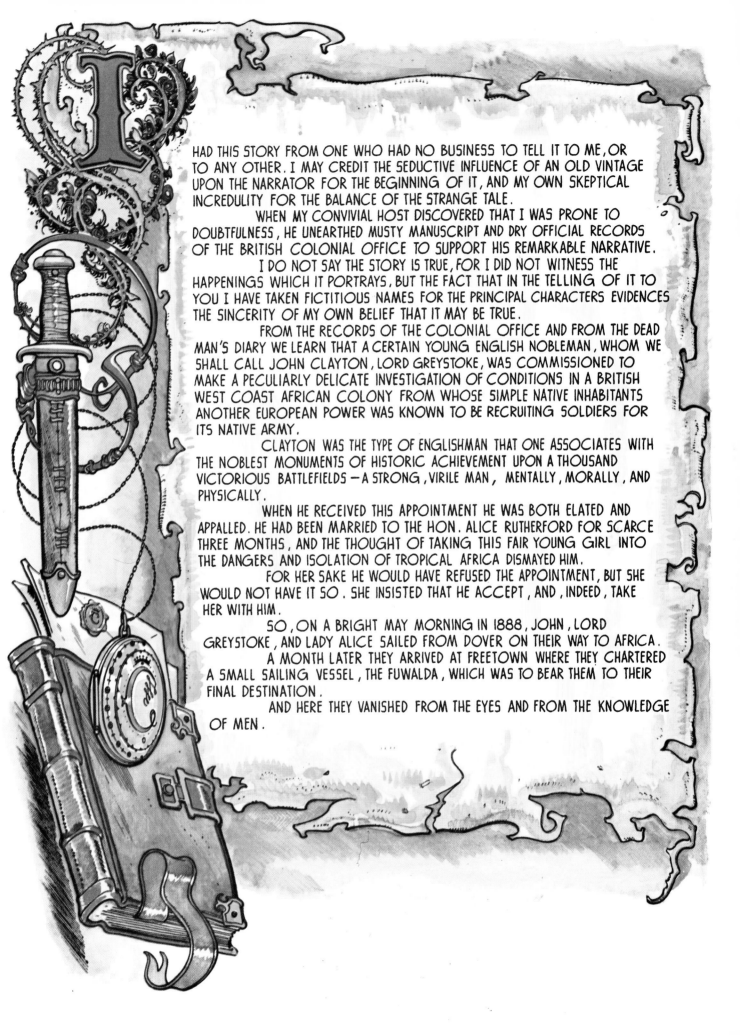

HAD THIS STORY FROM ONE WHO HAD NO BUSINESS TO TELL IT TO ME, OR TO ANY OTHER. I MAY CREDIT THE SEDUCTIVE INFLUENCE OF AN OLD VINTAGE UPON THE NARRATOR FOR THE BEGINNING OF IT, AND MY OWN SKEPTICAL INCREDULITY FOR THE BALANCE OF THE STRANGE TALE.

WHEN MY CONVIVIAL HOST DISCOVERED THAT I WAS PRONE TO DOUBTFULNESS, HE UNEARTHED MUSTY MANUSCRIPT AND DRY OFFICIAL RECORDS OF THE BRITISH COLONIAL OFFICE TO SUPPORT HIS REMARKABLE NARRATIVE.

I DO NOT SAY THE STORY IS TRUE, FOR I DID NOT WITNESS THE HAPPENINGS WHICH IT PORTRAYS, BUT THE FACT THAT IN THE TELLING OF IT TO YOU I HAVE TAKEN FICTITIOUS NAMES FOR THE PRINCIPAL CHARACTERS EVIDENCES THE SINCERITY OF MY OWN BELIEF THAT IT MAY BE TRUE.

FROM THE RECORDS OF THE COLONIAL OFFICE AND FROM THE DEAD MAN'S DIARY WE LEARN THAT A CERTAIN YOUNG ENGLISH NOBLEMAN, WHOM WE SHALL CALL JOHN CLAYTON, LORD GREYSTOKE, WAS COMMISSIONED TO MAKE A PECULIARLY DELICATE INVESTIGATION OF CONDITIONS IN A BRITISH WEST COAST AFRICAN COLONY FROM WHOSE SIMPLE NATIVE INHABITANTS ANOTHER EUROPEAN POWER WAS KNOWN TO BE RECRUITING SOLDIERS FOR ITS NATIVE ARMY.

CLAYTON WAS THE TYPE OF ENGLISHMAN THAT ONE ASSOCIATES WITH THE NOBLEST MONUMENTS OF HISTORIC ACHIEVEMENT UPON A THOUSAND VICTORIOUS BATTLEFIELDS — A STRONG, VIRILE MAN, MENTALLY, MORALLY, AND PHYSICALLY.

WHEN HE RECEIVED THIS APPOINTMENT HE WAS BOTH ELATED AND APPALLED. HE HAD BEEN MARRIED TO THE HON. ALICE RUTHERFORD FOR SCARCE THREE MONTHS, AND THE THOUGHT OF TAKING THIS FAIR YOUNG GIRL INTO THE DANGERS AND ISOLATION OF TROPICAL AFRICA DISMAYED HIM.

FOR HER SAKE HE WOULD HAVE REFUSED THE APPOINTMENT, BUT SHE WOULD NOT HAVE IT SO. SHE INSISTED THAT HE ACCEPT, AND, INDEED, TAKE HER WITH HIM.

SO, ON A BRIGHT MAY MORNING IN 1888, JOHN, LORD GREYSTOKE, AND LADY ALICE SAILED FROM DOVER ON THEIR WAY TO AFRICA.

A MONTH LATER THEY ARRIVED AT FREETOWN WHERE THEY CHARTERED A SMALL SAILING VESSEL, THE FUWALDA, WHICH WAS TO BEAR THEM TO THEIR FINAL DESTINATION.

AND HERE THEY VANISHED FROM THE EYES AND FROM THE KNOWLEDGE OF MEN.

THE FUWALDA,
A BARKENTINE OF
ABOUT ONE HUNDRED
TONS, WAS A VESSEL OF THE TYPE OFTEN
SEEN IN COASTWISE TRADE IN THE FAR
SOUTHERN ATLANTIC, THEIR CREWS COMPOSED
OF THE OFFSCOURINGS OF THE SEA ...
UNHANGED MURDERERS AND CUTTHROATS OF
EVERY RACE AND NATION. THE FUWALDA WAS NO
EXCEPTION TO THE RULE. HER OFFICERS WERE
BULLIES, HATING AND BEING HATED BY THEIR CREW.

THE CAPTAIN WAS
A BRUTE IN HIS
TREATMENT OF HIS MEN.
HE KNEW BUT TWO
ARGUMENTS IN HIS DEALINGS
WITH THEM — THE BELAYING PIN ...

...AND REVOLVER, NOR IS IT
LIKELY THAT THE MOTLEY
AGGREGATION HE
SIGNED WOULD HAVE
UNDERSTOOD
AUGHT ELSE.

SO IT WAS THAT FROM THE SECOND DAY OUT FROM FREETOWN JOHN CLAYTON AND HIS YOUNG WIFE WITNESSED SCENES UPON THE DECK OF THE FUWALDA SUCH AS THEY HAD BELIEVED WERE NEVER ENACTED OUTSIDE THE COVERS OF PRINTED STORIES OF THE SEA.

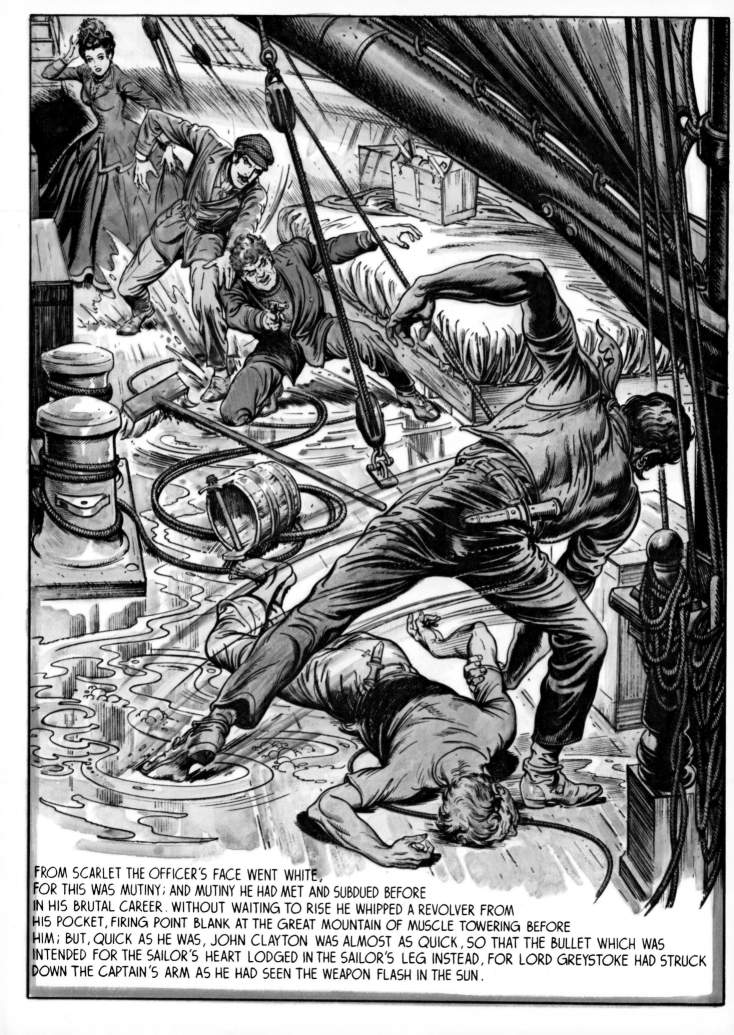

FROM SCARLET THE OFFICER'S FACE WENT WHITE,
FOR THIS WAS MUTINY; AND MUTINY HE HAD MET AND SUBDUED BEFORE
IN HIS BRUTAL CAREER. WITHOUT WAITING TO RISE HE WHIPPED A REVOLVER FROM
HIS POCKET, FIRING POINT BLANK AT THE GREAT MOUNTAIN OF MUSCLE TOWERING BEFORE
HIM; BUT, QUICK AS HE WAS, JOHN CLAYTON WAS ALMOST AS QUICK, SO THAT THE BULLET WHICH WAS
INTENDED FOR THE SAILOR'S HEART LODGED IN THE SAILOR'S LEG INSTEAD, FOR LORD GREYSTOKE HAD STRUCK
DOWN THE CAPTAIN'S ARM AS HE HAD SEEN THE WEAPON FLASH IN THE SUN.

WORDS PASSED BETWEEN CLAYTON AND THE CAPTAIN, THE FORMER MAKING IT PLAIN THAT HE WAS DISGUSTED WITH THE BRUTALITY DISPLAYED TOWARD THE CREW. THE CAPTAIN WAS ON THE POINT OF MAKING AN ANGRY REPLY, BUT, THINKING BETTER OF IT, TURNED ON HIS HEEL AND, BLACK AND SCOWLING, STRODE AFT.

BLACK MICHAEL TURNED TO CLAYTON WITH A WORD OF GRUFF THANKS. THE INCIDENT HAD ENDED...

...BUT THUS WAS FORGED THE FIRST LINK OF WHAT WAS DESTINED TO FORM A CHAIN OF CIRCUMSTANCES ENDING IN A LIFE OF ONE YET UNBORN SUCH AS HAS NEVER BEEN PARALLELED IN THE HISTORY OF MAN.

FOR SEVERAL DAYS THE CLAYTONS WERE LEFT VERY MUCH TO THEMSELVES. THIS IN ITSELF ISOLATED THEM FROM THE DAILY HAPPENINGS OF THE SHIP WHICH WERE SOON TO CULMINATE IN BLOODY TRAGEDY.

ONE MID-AFTERNOON, THE OLD SAILOR WHO HAD BEEN FELLED BY THE CAPTAIN CAME TO CLAYTON.

"MUTINY!" HE SAID, "THE CREW MEANS MUTINY AND MURDER. MARK MY WORD, IT'S COMIN', SIR."

"YOU HAVE BUT ONE DUTY, JOHN. IF YOU DO NOT WARN THE CAPTAIN YOU ARE AS MUCH A PARTY TO WHATEVER FOLLOWS AS THOUGH YOU HAD HELPED TO PLOT AND CARRY IT OUT WITH YOUR OWN HEAD AND HANDS."

"IT'S A LIE! AND IF YOU HAVE BEEN INTERFERING AGAIN WITH THE DISCIPLINE OF THIS SHIP OR MEDDLING IN AFFAIRS THAT DON'T CONCERN YOU, YOU CAN TAKE THE CONSEQUENCES, AND BE DAMNED."

"WELL, ALICE," SAID CLAYTON, AS HE REJOINED HIS WIFE, "I COULD HAVE SAVED MY BREATH. HE AND HIS BLASTED OLD SHIP MAY GO HANG, FOR AUGHT I CARE; AND UNTIL WE ARE SAFE OFF THE THING I SHALL SPEND MY ENERGIES IN LOOKING AFTER OUR OWN WELFARE."

RETURNING TO THEIR QUARTERS, THE CLAYTONS FOUND THE CABIN IN A STATE OF DISORDER. BOXES AND BAGS WERE STREWN ABOUT AND THE BEDS WERE TORN TO PIECES.

"ONLY THE REVOLVERS ARE MISSING, AND THE FACT THAT THEY WISHED FOR THEM ALONE IS THE MOST SINISTER CIRCUMSTANCE OF ALL THAT HAVE TRANSPIRED SINCE WE SET FOOT ON THIS MISERABLE HULK."

THEN, AS THEY FELL TO IN AN EFFORT TO STRAIGHTEN UP THEIR CABIN, THEY NOTICED A PIECE OF PAPER BEING SLIPPED UNDER THE DOOR OF THEIR QUARTERS.

QUICKLY AND SILENTLY CLAYTON STEPPED TOWARD THE DOOR, BUT, AS HE REACHED FOR THE KNOB TO THROW IT OPEN, HIS WIFE'S HAND FELL UPON HIS WRIST.

"NO, JOHN," SHE WHISPERED. "THEY DO NOT WISH TO BE SEEN, AND SO WE CANNOT AFFORD TO SEE THEM."

"POSSIBLY OUR BEST CHANCE FOR SALVATION LIES IN MAINTAINING A NEUTRAL POSITION."

CLAYTON DROPPED HIS HAND TO HIS SIDE.

THUS THEY STOOD WATCHING THE LITTLE BIT OF WHITE PAPER UNTIL IT FINALLY REMAINED AT REST UPON THE FLOOR JUST INSIDE THE DOOR. THEN CLAYTON STOOPED AND PICKED IT UP.

KEEP YOUR MOUTHS SHUT—YOU TELL THE CAPTAIN ONE WORD ABOUT THIS AND YOU ARE DEAD!

THE NEXT MORNING, A SIGHT MET CLAYTON'S EYES WHICH CONFIRMED HIS WORST FEARS. FACING A KNOT OF OFF-ICERS WAS THE FUWALDA'S CREW, LED BY BLACK MICHAEL. AT THE FIRST VOLLEY FROM THE OFFICERS . . .

. . . THE MEN RAN FOR SHELTER, AND FROM POINTS OF VANTAGE BEHIND MASTS, WHEELHOUSE, AND CABIN THEY RETURNED THE FIRE OF THE FIVE MEN WHO REPRESENTED THE HATED AUTHORITY OF THE SHIP.

BUT AT A CRY OF COMMAND FROM BLACK MICHAEL, THE BLOOD-THIRSTY RUFFIANS, MOST OF THEM ARMED WITH BOAT HOOKS, HATCHETS AND CROWBARS, CHARGED THE OFFICERS.

IN THE INFURIATED RUSH THE CAPTAIN WAS CUT DOWN AND AN INSTANT LATER THE OTHERS WERE DOWN, DEAD OR WOUNDED FROM DOZENS OF BLOWS AND BULLET WOUNDS. SHORT AND GRISLY WAS THE WORK OF THE MUTINEERS.

NOW WITHOUT COMPASSION THEY PROCEEDED TO THROW BOTH DEAD AND DYING OVER THE SIDES OF THE VESSEL.

THROUGH IT ALL THE CLAYTONS STOOD ASIDE. NOW ONE OF THE CREW SPIED THEM. "HERE'S TWO MORE FOR THE FISHES, HE CRIED, AND RUSHED TOWARD THEM WITH UPLIFTED AX.

BUT BLACK MICHAEL WAS EVEN QUICKER.
SCARCE HAD THE FELLOW TAKEN A HALF DOZEN
STEPS WHEN HE WENT DOWN WITH A BULLET IN HIS BACK.

WITH A ROAR BLACK MICHAEL
TURNED TO THE OTHERS. "THESE HERE ARE MY FRIENDS.
THEY'RE TO BE LEFT ALONE. I'M CAPTAIN OF
THIS SHIP NOW, AN' WHAT I SAY GOES!"

ON THE FIFTH DAY FOLLOWING THE MURDER OF THE OFFICERS, LAND WAS SIGHTED. HERE, IF THE PLACE WAS HABITABLE, LORD AND LADY GREYSTOKE WERE TO BE PUT ASHORE.

BEFORE THE DARK THE BARKENTINE LAY PEACEFULLY AT ANCHOR UPON THE BOSOM OF THE STILL, MIRRORLIKE SURFACE OF THE HARBOR. THE SURROUNDING SHORES WERE BEAUTIFUL WITH SEMITROPICAL VERDURE, WHILE IN THE DISTANCE THE COUNTRY ROSE FROM THE OCEAN IN HILL AND TABLELAND, ALMOST UNIFORMLY CLOTHED BY PRIMEVAL FOREST.

AS DARKNESS SETTLED UPON THE EARTH, CLAYTON AND LADY ALICE STILL STOOD BY THE SHIP'S RAIL IN SILENT CONTEMPLATION OF THEIR FUTURE ABODE.

FROM THE DARK SHADOWS OF THE MIGHTY FOREST CAME THE WILD CALLS OF SAVAGE BEASTS — THE DEEP ROAR OF THE LION AND, OCCASIONALLY, THE SHRILL SCREAMS OF A PANTHER.

LATER IN THE EVENING BLACK MICHAEL JOINED THEM LONG ENOUGH TO INSTRUCT THEM TO MAKE THEIR PREPARATIONS FOR LANDING ON THE MORROW.

THEY TRIED TO PERSUADE HIM TO TAKE THEM TO SOME MORE HOSPITABLE COAST NEAR ENOUGH TO CIVILIZATION SO THAT THEY MIGHT HOPE TO FALL INTO FRIENDLY HANDS. BUT NO PLEAS, OR THREATS, OR PROMISES OF REWARD COULD MOVE HIM.

"I AM THE ONLY MAN ABOARD WHO WOULD NOT RATHER SEE YOU BOTH SAFELY DEAD, YET BLACK MICHAEL'S NOT THE MAN TO FORGET A FAVOR. YOU SAVED MY LIFE ONCE, AND IN RETURN I'M GOIN' TO SPARE YOURS, BUT THAT'S ALL I CAN DO."

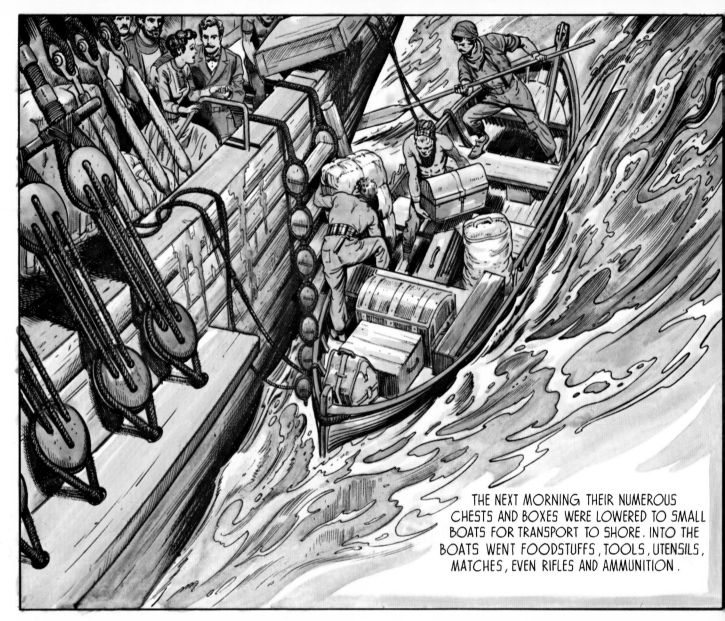

THE NEXT MORNING THEIR NUMEROUS CHESTS AND BOXES WERE LOWERED TO SMALL BOATS FOR TRANSPORT TO SHORE. INTO THE BOATS WENT FOODSTUFFS, TOOLS, UTENSILS, MATCHES, EVEN RIFLES AND AMMUNITION.

BLACK MICHAEL ACCOMPANIED THEM TO SHORE, AND WAS LAST TO LEAVE WHEN THE BOATS, THEIR CASKS FILLED WITH FRESH WATER, SHOVED OUT TO THE WAITING FUWALDA.

CLAYTON AND HIS WIFE STOOD SILENTLY WATCHING THEIR DEPARTURE WITH A FEELING OF UTTER HOPELESSNESS.

AS THEY WATCHED THE FUWALDA PASS THROUGH THE HARBOR AND OUT OF SIGHT, LADY ALICE BURST INTO UNCONTROLLABLE SOBS. BRAVELY SHE HAD FACED THE DANGERS OF THE MUTINY. NOW HER NERVES GAVE WAY, AND THE REACTION CAME.

"HUNDREDS OF THOUSANDS OF YEARS AGO, OUR ANCESTORS OF THE DIM AND DISTANT PAST FACED THE SAME PROBLEMS WE MUST FACE POSSIBLY IN THESE SAME PRIMEVAL FORESTS.

THAT WE ARE HERE TODAY EVIDENCES THEIR VICTORY. WHAT THEY ACCOMPLISHED, ALICE, WITH INSTRUMENTS AND WEAPONS OF STONE AND BONE, SURELY THAT WE MAY ACCOMPLISH, ALSO."

"THERE IS ONE THING TO DO. WORK MUST BE OUR SALVATION." "BUT JOHN, IF IT WERE ONLY YOU AND ME," SHE SOBBED, "WE COULD ENDURE IT I KNOW; BUT ..."

CLAYTON'S FIRST THOUGHT WAS
TO ARRANGE A SLEEPING SHELTER
FOR THE NIGHT, SOMETHING
WHICH MIGHT SERVE TO PROTECT
THEM FROM PROWLING
BEASTS OF PREY.

ALL DURING THE DAY
THE FOREST ABOUT THEM
HAD BEEN FILLED WITH EXCITED
BIRDS OF BRILLIANT PLUMAGE, AND
DANCING, CHATTERING MONKEYS
WHO WATCHED THESE NEW
ARRIVALS AND THEIR WONDERFUL
NEST-BUILDING OPERATIONS
WITH EVERY MARK OF KEENEST
INTEREST AND FASCINATION.

IT WAS NOW LATE IN THE
AFTERNOON, AND THE BALANCE OF
THE DAYLIGHT HOURS WERE DEVOTED TO
THE BUILDING OF A RUDE LADDER BY
MEANS OF WHICH LADY ALICE COULD
MOUNT TO HER NEW HOME.

AND BEHIND THEM ALL, OVER THE EDGE OF A LOW RIDGE, OTHER EYES WATCHED — CLOSE-SET, WICKED EYES, GLEAMING BENEATH SHAGGY BROWS.

SUDDENLY ALICE, STRAINING HER EYES INTO THE DARKENING SHADOWS, GRASPED HER HUSBAND'S ARM. "JOHN," SHE WHISPERED. CLAYTON TURNED. "LOOK! WHAT IS IT, A MAN?"

SILHOUETTED DIMLY AGAINST THE SHADOWS BEYOND, WAS A GREAT FIGURE STANDING UPRIGHT. MOMENTARILY IT STOOD AS THOUGH LISTENING, THEN IT MELTED INTO THE SHADOWS OF THE JUNGLE.

EXHAUSTED, THEY LAY DOWN WITHIN THEIR TINY AERIE TO TRY TO GAIN, THROUGH SLEEP, A BRIEF RESPITE OF FORGETFULNESS. CLAYTON LAY FACING FRONT, RIFLE AND REVOLVERS READY AT HAND.

THEY HAD SCARCE CLOSED THEIR EYES, WHEN THE TERRIFYING CRY OF A PANTHER RANG OUT. THEY COULD HEAR THE BEAST SNIFFING AND CLAWING AT THE TREES BELOW THE PLATFORM. AT LAST IT ROAMED AWAY, A GREAT, HANDSOME BEAST, THE LARGEST CLAYTON HAD EVER SEEN.

DURING THE LONG HOURS OF DARKNESS THE NIGHT NOISES OF THE JUNGLE KEPT THEIR OVERWROUGHT NERVES ON EDGE, AND THEIR FITFUL SNATCHES OF SLEEP WERE LACED BY PIERCING SCREAMS AND THE MOVING OF STEALTHY BODIES BENEATH THEM.

MORNING FOUND THEM BUT LITTLE REFRESHED, THOUGH IT WAS WITH A FEELING OF INTENSE RELIEF THAT THEY SAW THE DAY DAWN. AS SOON AS THEY HAD MADE THEIR MEAGER BREAKFAST OF SALT PORK, COFFEE, AND BISCUIT, CLAYTON COMMENCED WORK UPON THEIR HOUSE. THE TASK WAS AN ARDUOUS ONE AND REQUIRED THE BETTER PART OF A MONTH, THOUGH HE BUILT BUT ONE SMALL ROOM. HE CONSTRUCTED HIS CABIN OF SMALL LOGS, STOPPING THE CHINKS WITH CLAY. AT ONE END HE BUILT A FIREPLACE OF SMALL STONES FROM THE BEACH.

IN THE WINDOW OPENING HE SET BRANCHES, SO WOVEN THAT THEY FORMED A SUBSTANTIAL GRATING THAT COULD WITHSTAND THE STRENGTH OF A POWERFUL ANIMAL. THE DOOR HE BUILT OF PIECES OF THE PACKING BOXES WHICH HAD HELD THEIR BELONGINGS, NAILING ONE PIECE UPON ANOTHER UNTIL HE HAD A SOLID BODY OF GREAT STRENGTH, HUNG ON TWO MASSIVE HARDWOOD HINGES. THE BUILDING OF A BED, CHAIRS, TABLE, AND SHELVES WAS A RELATIVELY EASY MATTER, SO THAT BY THE END OF THE SECOND MONTH THEY WERE WELL SETTLED, AND, BUT FOR THE CONSTANT DREAD OF ATTACK BY WILD BEASTS AND THE EVER GROW-ING LONELINESS, THEY WERE NOT UNCOMFORTABLE OR UNHAPPY.

AT NIGHT GREAT BEASTS SNARLED ABOUT THEIR TINY CABIN, BUT NOW THEY PAID LITTLE ATTENTION TO THEM, SLEEPING SOUNDLY THE WHOLE NIGHT THROUGH.

THRICE THEY HAD CAUGHT FLEETING GLIMPSES OF GREAT MAN-LIKE FIGURES, BUT NEVER AT SUFFICIENTLY CLOSE RANGE TO KNOW WHETHER THESE WERE MAN OR BRUTE.

BUT ONE AFTERNOON, WHILE CLAYTON WAS WORKING ON AN ADDITION TO THEIR CABIN, A NUMBER OF FRIGHTENED MONKEYS CAME SHRIEKING THROUGH THE TREES FROM THE DIRECTION OF THE RIDGE, AS THOUGH TO WARN HIM OF APPROACHING DANGER.

AT LAST HE SAW IT, THE THING THE MONKEYS FEARED— THE MAN-BRUTE OF WHICH THE CLAYTONS HAD CAUGHT OCCASIONAL FLEETING GLIMPSES. IT WAS APPROACHING THROUGH THE JUNGLE—A GREAT ANTHROPOID APE, AND AS IT ADVANCED, IT EMITTED DEEP GUTTERAL GROWLS AND A LOW BARKING SOUND.

CLAYTON WAS SOME DISTANCE FROM THE CABIN, ARMED ONLY WITH AN AX.

NOW THE GREAT APE CAME CRASHING DIRECTLY TOWARD HIM—AND FROM A POINT WHICH PRACTICALLY CUT OFF HIS ESCAPE. HIS CHANCES WITH THIS MONSTER WERE SMALL INDEED.

ALICE, WHAT WOULD BECOME OF ALICE? YET THERE WAS STILL A SLIGHT CHANCE OF REACHING THE CABIN. HE TURNED AND RAN, SHOUTING AN ALARM TO HIS WIFE.

LADY GREYSTOKE, HEARING THE CRY, LOOKED UP TO SEE THE APE SPRINGING WITH INCREDIBLE SWIFTNESS. WITH A LOW CRY SHE SPRANG TOWARD THE CABIN, HER SOUL FILLED WITH TERROR, FOR THE BRUTE HAD INTERCEPTED HER HUSBAND. HE STOOD AT BAY, GRASPING HIS AX, READY TO SWING SHOULD THE INFURIATED ANIMAL MAKE HIS FINAL CHARGE. "CLOSE AND BOLT THE DOOR, ALICE," HE CRIED. "I CAN FINISH THIS FELLOW OFF WITH MY AX."

BUT HE KNEW HE WAS FACING A HORRIBLE DEATH, AND SO DID SHE. THE APE, A GREAT BULL, BARED HIS FANGS IN A HORRID SNARL AND HIS EYES GLEAMED HATRED AS HE PAUSED A MOMENT BEFORE HIS PREY. OVER THE BRUTE'S SHOULDER CLAYTON SAW HIS WIFE EMERGE FROM THE CABIN, ARMED WITH A RIFLE.

HORROR AND FEAR SEIZED HIM. SHE HAD ALWAYS BEEN AFRAID OF FIREARMS, BUT NOW SHE RUSHED TOWARD THE APE FEARLESSLY LIKE A LIONESS PROTECTING ITS YOUNG.

"ALICE," SHOUTED CLAYTON, "FOR GOD'S SAKE, GO BACK!"

BUT JUST THEN THE APE CHARGED AND THE MAN SWUNG THE AX WITH ALL HIS MIGHT. THE POWERFUL BRUTE TORE IT FROM CLAYTON'S GRASP.

WITH AN UGLY SNARL, HE CLOSED UPON HIS DEFENSELESS VICTIM. BUT ERE HIS FANGS HAD REACHED THE THROAT THEY THIRSTED FOR...

...THERE WAS A SHARP REPORT AND A BULLET ENTERED THE APE'S BACK BETWEEN HIS SHOULDERS.

THROWING CLAYTON TO THE GROUND, THE BEAST TURNED UPON HIS NEW ENEMY. BEFORE SHE COULD FIRE ANOTHER BULLET, THE BRUTE LUNGED.

ALMOST AT ONCE, LORD GREYSTOKE REGAINED HIS FEET AND RUSHED FORWARD TO DRAG THE APE FROM HIS WIFE'S PROSTRATE FORM.

TO HIS SURPRISE, THE GREAT BULK ROLLED INERTLY UPON THE TURF.

THE BULLET HAD DONE ITS WORK. THE APE WAS DEAD.

A HASTY EXAMINATION OF HIS WIFE REVEALED NO MARKS UPON HER, AND CLAYTON DECIDED THAT THE BRUTE HAD DIED THE INSTANT HE HAD SPRUNG.

GENTLY HE LIFTED HIS WIFE'S STILL UNCONSCIOUS FORM AND BORE HER TO THE LITTLE CABIN. IT WAS TWO HOURS BEFORE SHE REGAINED CONSCIOUSNESS.

BUT HER FIRST WORDS FILLED CLAYTON WITH APPREHENSION. "OH, JOHN, I'VE HAD AN AWFUL DREAM. I THOUGHT WE WEREN'T IN LONDON, BUT IN SOME AWFUL PLACE WHERE WILD BEASTS ATTACKED US." "THERE, THERE, ALICE," HE SAID. "TRY TO SLEEP AGAIN. DO NOT WORRY ABOUT BAD DREAMS."

AND THAT NIGHT A LITTLE SON WAS BORN IN THE TINY CABIN BESIDE THE PRIMEVAL FOREST WHILE A LEOPARD
SCREAMED BEFORE THE DOOR AND THE DEEP NOTES OF A LION'S ROAR SOUNDED FROM BEYOND THE RIDGE.

LADY GREYSTOKE NEVER RECOVERED FROM THE SHOCK OF THE GREAT APE'S ATTACK. NOW THAT THE BABY WAS BORN, SHE NEVER VENTURED AGAIN OUTSIDE THE CABIN, NOR DID SHE EVER REALIZE SHE WAS NOT IN ENGLAND.

IN OTHER WAYS SHE WAS QUITE RATIONAL, AND THE JOY SHE TOOK IN HER LITTLE SON AND THE CONSTANT ATTENTIONS OF HER HUSBAND MADE THAT YEAR THE HAPPIEST OF HER YOUNG LIFE.

CLAYTON HAD LONG SINCE GIVEN UP ANY HOPE OF RESCUE, SO THAT WHILE HE SUFFERED TERRIBLY TO SEE HER SO, YET HE WAS ALMOST GLAD SHE COULD NOT UNDERSTAND.

WITH UNREMITTING ZEAL, HE WORKED TO BEAUTIFY AND STRENGTHEN THE CABIN.

DURING THE YEAR THAT FOLLOWED, CLAYTON WAS SEVERAL TIMES ATTACKED BY THE GREAT APES WHICH NOW SEEMED TO CONTINUALLY INFEST THE VICINITY OF THE CABIN ; BUT AS HE NEVER AGAIN VENTURED OUTSIDE WITHOUT BOTH RIFLE AND REVOLVERS , HE HAD LITTLE FEAR OF THE HUGE BEASTS.

IN HIS LEISURE CLAYTON READ ALOUD TO HIS WIFE FROM THE STORE OF BOOKS HE HAD BROUGHT. AMONG THESE WERE PICTURE BOOKS, PRIMERS, READERS FOR CHILDREN SINCE THEY HAD KNOWN THEIR CHILD WOULD BE OLD ENOUGH FOR SUCH BEFORE THEY MIGHT HOPE TO RETURN TO ENGLAND.

AT OTHER TIMES , CLAYTON WROTE IN HIS DIARY, WHICH HE HAD ALWAYS BEEN ACCUSTOMED TO KEEP IN FRENCH ...

... AND IN WHICH HE RECORDED THE DETAILS OF THEIR STRANGE LIFE. THIS BOOK HE KEPT LOCKED IN A LITTLE METAL BOX.

A YEAR FROM THE DAY HER LITTLE
SON WAS BORN, LADY ALICE PASSED QUIETLY
AWAY IN THE NIGHT. SO PEACEFUL WAS HER END THAT
IT WAS HOURS BEFORE CLAYTON COULD AWAKE TO
A REALIZATION THAT HIS WIFE WAS DEAD.

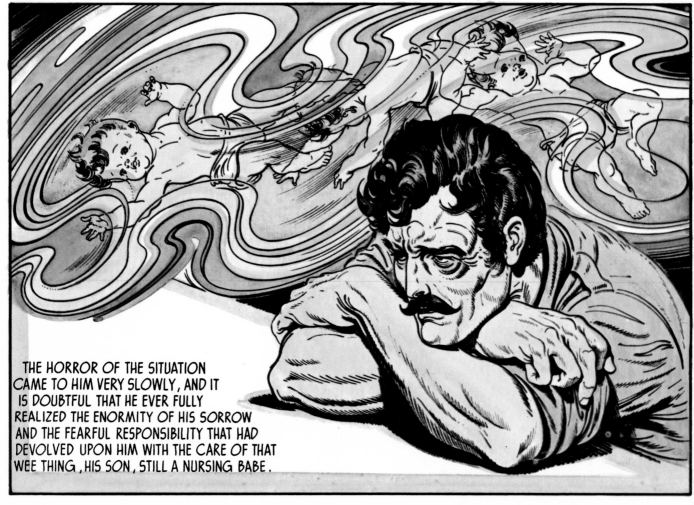

THE HORROR OF THE SITUATION
CAME TO HIM VERY SLOWLY, AND IT
IS DOUBTFUL THAT HE EVER FULLY
REALIZED THE ENORMITY OF HIS SORROW
AND THE FEARFUL RESPONSIBILITY THAT HAD
DEVOLVED UPON HIM WITH THE CARE OF THAT
WEE THING, HIS SON, STILL A NURSING BABE.

THE LAST ENTRY IN HIS DIARY WAS MADE THE
MORNING FOLLOWING HER DEATH, AND THERE HE RECITES THE SAD DETAILS IN A MATTER-
OF-FACT WAY THAT ADDS TO THE PATHOS OF IT; FOR IT BREATHES A TIRED APATHY BORN OF LONG SORROW
AND HOPELESSNESS, WHICH EVEN THIS CRUEL BLOW COULD SCARCELY AWAKE TO FURTHER SUFFERING: "MY LITTLE
SON IS CRYING FOR NOURISHMENT—O, ALICE, ALICE, WHAT SHALL I DO?" AND AS JOHN CLAYTON WROTE THESE
LAST WORDS, HE DROPPED HIS HEAD WEARILY TO HIS OUTSTRETCHED ARMS UPON THE TABLE HE HAD BUILT FOR HER
WHO LAY COLD AND STILL IN THE BED BESIDE HIM.

FOR A LONG TIME
NO SOUND BROKE THE
DEATHLIKE STILLNESS OF THE
JUNGLE MIDDAY SAVE THE PITEOUS
WAILING OF THE TINY MAN-CHILD.

KERCHAK WAS A HUGE KING APE, WEIGHING PERHAPS THREE HUNDRED AND FIFTY POUNDS. HIS FOREHEAD WAS EXTREMELY LOW AND RECEDING, HIS EYES BLOODSHOT, SMALL AND CLOSE-SET TO HIS COARSE, FLAT NOSE; HIS EARS LARGE AND THIN, BUT SMALLER THAN MOST OF HIS KIND. HIS AWFUL TEMPER AND HIS MIGHTY STRENGTH MADE HIM SUPREME AMONG THE LITTLE TRIBE INTO WHICH HE HAD BEEN BORN SOME TWENTY YEARS BEFORE.

NOW THAT HE WAS IN HIS PRIME, THERE WAS NO SIMIAN IN ALL THE MIGHTY FOREST THROUGH WHICH HE ROVED THAT DARED CONTEST HIS RIGHT TO RULE.

OLD TANTOR, THE ELEPHANT, ALONE OF ALL THE WILD SAVAGE LIFE, FEARED HIM NOT—AND HE ALONE DID KERCHAK FEAR.

THE TRIBE OF ANTHROPOIDS OVER WHICH KERCHAK RULED WITH AN IRON HAND AND BARED FANGS, NUMBERED SOME SIX OR EIGHT FAMILIES, EACH FAMILY CONSISTING OF AN ADULT MALE WITH HIS WIVES AND THEIR YOUNG, NUMBERING IN ALL SOME SIXTY OR SEVENTY APES.

KALA WAS THE YOUNGEST WIFE OF A MALE NAMED TUBLAT, MEANING BROKEN NOSE, AND HER CHILD WAS HER FIRST, FOR SHE WAS BUT NINE OR TEN YEARS OLD.

NOTWITHSTANDING HER YOUTH, SHE WAS LARGE AND POWERFUL—A SPLENDID, CLEAN-LIMBED ANIMAL, WITH A ROUND, HIGH FOREHEAD WHICH DENOTED MORE INTELLIGENCE THAN MOST OF HER KIND POSSESSED. SO, ALSO, SHE HAD A GREATER CAPACITY FOR MOTHER LOVE AND MOTHER SORROW.

NOW, IN THE FOREST OF THE TABLELAND A MILE BACK FROM THE OCEAN, KERCHAK WAS ON A RAMPAGE OF RAGE AMONG HIS PEOPLE. THE YOUNGER AND LIGHTER MEMBERS OF HIS TRIBE SCAMPERED TO THE HIGHER BRANCHES OF THE GREAT TREES TO ESCAPE HIS WRATH, RISKING THEIR LIVES UPON BRANCHES THAT SCARCE SUPPORTED THEIR WEIGHT RATHER THAN FACE OLD KERCHAK IN ONE OF HIS FITS OF UNCONTROLLED ANGER. THE OTHER MALES SCATTERED...

...BUT NOT BEFORE THE INFURIATED BRUTE HAD FELT THE VERTEBRA OF ONE SNAP BETWEEN HIS GREAT, FOAMING JAWS.

THEN HE SPIED KALA, WHO, RETURNING FROM A SEARCH FOR FOOD WITH HER YOUNG BABE, WAS IGNORANT OF KERCHAK'S TEMPER UNTIL SUDDENLY SHRILL WARNINGS CAUSED HER TO SCAMPER MADLY FOR SAFETY.

BUT KERCHAK WAS CLOSE UPON HER, SO CLOSE THAT HE HAD ALMOST GRASPED HER ANKLE HAD SHE NOT MADE A FURIOUS LEAP FAR INTO SPACE FROM ONE TREE TO ANOTHER.

SHE MADE THE LEAP SUCCESSFULLY, BUT AS SHE GRASPED THE LIMB OF THE FURTHER TREE, THE SUDDEN JAR LOOSENED THE HOLD OF THE TINY BABE WHERE IT CLUNG FRANTICALLY TO HER NECK, AND SHE SAW THE LITTLE THING HURLED, TURNING AND TWISTING, TO THE GROUND THIRTY FEET BELOW.

WITH A LOW CRY OF DISMAY,
KALA RUSHED HEADLONG TO ITS SIDE,
THOUGHTLESS NOW OF THE DANGER FROM KERCHAK;
BUT WHEN SHE GATHERED THE WEE, MANGLED FORM TO HER
BOSOM LIFE HAD LEFT IT. WITH LOW MOANS, SHE SAT CUDDLING THE BODY
TO HER; NOR DID KERCHAK ATTEMPT TO MOLEST HER. WITH THE DEATH OF THE BABE,
HIS FIT OF DEMONIACAL RAGE PASSED AS SUDDENLY AS IT HAD SEIZED HIM.

WHEN THE TRIBE SAW THAT KERCHAK'S RAGE HAD
CEASED, THEY CAME SLOWLY DOWN FROM THEIR AR-
BOREAL RETREATS AND PURSUED AGAIN THE VARIOUS
OCCUPATIONS WHICH HE HAD INTERRUPTED. THEY HAD
PASSED AN HOUR OR SO THUS WHEN KERCHAK CALLED
THEM TOGETHER AND, WITH A WORD OF COMMAND TO
THEM TO FOLLOW HIM, SET OFF TOWARD THE SEA.

ALL THE WAY, KALA CARRIED HER LITTLE DEAD BABY CLOSE TO HER BREAST.
SHORTLY AFTER NOON, THEY REACHED THE BEACH WHERE LAY THE TINY COTTAGE
WHICH WAS KERCHAK'S GOAL. KERCHAK HAD MADE UP HIS MIND TO EXPLORE THE INTERIOR OF THAT
MYSTERIOUS DEN, AND HE WANTED THE LITTLE BLACK STICK THAT MADE A LOUD NOISE AND BROUGHT DEATH
FROM THE HANDS OF THE STRANGE WHITE APE.

TODAY THERE WAS NO SIGN
OF THE MAN ABOUT. SLOWLY,
CAUTIOUSLY, THEY CREPT TOWARD
THE LITTLE CABIN. THE DOOR
WAS OPEN.

ON THEY CAME. KERCHAK, AND BEHIND HIM
TWO MALES, THEN KALA, STRAINING THE LITTLE
DEAD FORM TO HER BREAST.

KERCHAK HIMSELF
SLUNK STEALTHILY TO
THE VERY DOOR AND
PEERED WITHIN.

THE SIGHT THAT
MET CLAYTON'S EYES
FROZE HIM WITH
HORROR.

INSIDE THE DEN THEY SAW THE STRANGE
WHITE APE LYING HALF ACROSS A TABLE,
HIS HEAD BURIED IN HIS ARMS; AND ON
THE BED LAY A FIGURE COVERED BY A SAIL-
CLOTH, WHILE FROM A TINY RUSTIC
CRADLE CAME THE PLAINTIVE WAILING OF
A BABE. NOISELESSLY THEY ENTERED.

KERCHAK STRUCK, AND WHEN HE RELEASED THE LIMP FORM WHICH HAD BEEN LORD GREYSTOKE HE TURNED HIS ATTENTION TO THE CRADLE.

BUT KALA WAS THERE BEFORE HIM. BEFORE HE COULD GRASP THE CHILD, SHE SNATCHED THE LIVE BABY OF LADY ALICE, DROPPED THE DEAD BABY OF HER OWN IN THE CRADLE, AND BOLTED THROUGH THE DOOR.

HIGH AMONG THE TREES SHE HUGGED THE SHRIEKING INFANT TO HER BOSOM, AND SOON THE IN-STINCT THAT WAS DOMINANT IN THIS FIERCE FEMALE REACHED OUT TO THE TINY MAN-CHILD AND HE BECAME QUIET. THEN HUNGER CLOSED THE GAP BETWEEN THEM AND THE SON OF AN ENGLISH LORD AND LADY NURSED AT THE BREAST OF KALA, THE GREAT APE.

SATISFIED THE TWO CLAYTONS WERE DEAD, KERCHAK PAUSED BEFORE THE DEATH-DEALING THUNDERSTICK ON THE WALL. CAUTIOUSLY HE REGARDED IT.

NOW IT WAS IN HIS HAND. HE FELT OF IT FROM END TO END, PEERED DOWN ITS MIDDLE, FINGERED THE BREECH, AND FINALLY THE TRIGGER.

THERE WAS A DEAFENING ROAR AND THE APES FELL OVER ONE ANOTHER IN THEIR WILD ANXIETY TO ESCAPE.

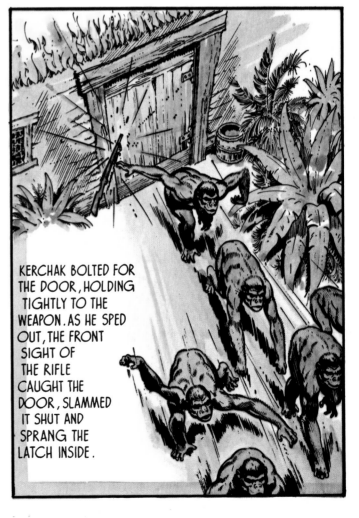

KERCHAK BOLTED FOR THE DOOR, HOLDING TIGHTLY TO THE WEAPON. AS HE SPED OUT, THE FRONT SIGHT OF THE RIFLE CAUGHT THE DOOR, SLAMMED IT SHUT AND SPRANG THE LATCH INSIDE.

IT WAS AN HOUR BEFORE
THE APES COULD AGAIN
BRING THEMSELVES TO
APPROACH THE CABIN,
AND WHEN THEY FINALLY DID SO,
THEY FOUND THAT THE DOOR WAS
SO SECURELY FASTENED THAT THEY
COULD NOT FORCE IT. THE CLEVERLY
CONSTRUCTED LATCH WHICH CLAYTON HAD MADE
HAD SPRUNG AS KERCHAK PASSED OUT; NOR COULD THE APES
FIND MEANS OF INGRESS THROUGH THE HEAVILY BARRED WINDOWS.

AFTER ROAMING ABOUT THE VICINITY FOR A SHORT TIME, THEY STARTED BACK
FOR THE DEEPER FORESTS AND THE HIGHER LAND FROM WHENCE THEY HAD COME.

KALA HAD NOT ONCE COME TO EARTH WITH HER LITTLE ADOPTED BABE, BUT NOW KERCHAK CALLED TO HER TO DESCEND, AND AS THERE WAS NO NOTE OF ANGER IN HIS VOICE SHE JOINED THE OTHERS ON THE HOMEWARD MARCH.

ON THE JOURNEY, SHE CLUNG DESPERATELY TO THE NEW BABE. SHE HAD SEEN ONE CHILD FALL TO A TERRIBLE DEATH AND SHE WOULD TAKE NO CHANCES WITH THIS ONE. THOSE OF THE APES WHO ATTEMPTED TO EXAMINE KALA'S STRANGE BABY WERE REPULSED WITH BARED FANGS AND LOW GROWLS, ACCOMPANIED BY WORDS OF WARNING FROM KALA.

TENDERLY KALA NURSED HER LITTLE WAIF, WONDERING SILENTLY WHY IT DID NOT GAIN STRENGTH AND AGILITY AS DID THE LITTLE APES OF OTHER MOTHERS. IT WAS NEARLY A YEAR FROM THE TIME THE LITTLE FELLOW CAME INTO HER POSSESSION BEFORE HE WOULD WALK ALONE, AND AS FOR CLIMBING — MY, BUT HOW STUPID HE WAS!

KALA SOMETIMES TALKED WITH THE OLDER FEMALES ABOUT HER YOUNG HOPEFUL, BUT NONE OF THEM COULD UNDERSTAND HOW A CHILD COULD BE SO SLOW AND BACKWARD IN LEARNING TO CARE FOR ITSELF. WHY, IT COULD NOT EVEN FIND FOOD ALONE, AND MORE THAN TWELVE MOONS HAD PASSED SINCE KALA HAD COME UPON IT.

HAD THEY KNOWN THAT THE CHILD HAD SEEN THIRTEEN MOONS BEFORE IT CAME INTO KALA'S POSSESSION, THEY WOULD HAVE CONSIDERED ITS CASE AS ABSOLUTELY HOPELESS, FOR THE LITTLE APES OF THEIR OWN TRIBE WERE AS FAR ADVANCED IN TWO OR THREE MOONS AS WAS THIS LITTLE STRANGER AFTER TWENTY-FIVE.

TUBLAT, KALA'S HUSBAND, WAS SORELY VEXED, AND BUT FOR THE FEMALE'S CAREFUL WATCHING, WOULD HAVE PUT THE CHILD OUT OF THE WAY. "HE WILL NEVER BE A GREAT APE," HE ARGUED. "ALWAYS WILL YOU HAVE TO CARRY HIM AND PROTECT HIM. WHAT GOOD WILL HE BE TO THE TRIBE? NONE; ONLY A BURDEN. LET US LEAVE HIM QUIETLY SLEEPING AMONG THE TALL GRASSES, THAT YOU MAY BEAR OTHER AND STRONGER APES TO GUARD US IN OUR OLD AGE." "NEVER, BROKEN NOSE," REPLIED KALA. "IF I MUST CARRY HIM FOREVER, SO BE IT."

AND THEN TUBLAT WENT TO KERCHAK TO URGE HIM TO USE HIS AUTHORITY WITH KALA AND FORCE HER TO GIVE UP LITTLE TARZAN, WHICH WAS THE NAME THEY HAD GIVEN TO THE TINY LORD GREYSTOKE, AND WHICH MEANT "WHITE SKIN." BUT WHEN KERCHAK SPOKE TO HER ABOUT IT, KALA THREATENED TO RUN AWAY FROM THE TRIBE IF THEY DID NOT LEAVE HER IN PEACE WITH THE CHILD.

AS TARZAN GREW, HE MADE RAPID STRIDES, SO THAT BY THE TIME HE WAS TEN YEARS OLD HE WAS AN EXCELLENT CLIMBER AND COULD DO MANY WONDERFUL THINGS WHICH WERE BEYOND THE POWERS OF HIS BROTHERS AND SISTERS.

IN MANY WAYS DID HE DIFFER FROM THEM, AND THEY OFTEN MARVELED AT HIS SUPERIOR CUNNING, BUT IN STRENGTH AND SIZE HE WAS DEFICIENT; FOR AT TEN THE GREAT ANTHROPOIDS WERE FULLY GROWN, SOME OF THEM TOWERING OVER SIX FEET IN HEIGHT... WHILE TARZAN WAS STILL BUT A HALF GROWN BOY.

YET SUCH A BOY! FROM EARLY INFANCY HE HAD USED HIS HANDS TO SWING FROM BRANCH TO BRANCH AFTER THE MANNER OF HIS GIANT MOTHER, AND AS HE GREW OLDER HE SPENT HOUR UPON HOUR DAILY SPEEDING THROUGH THE TREE TOPS. HE COULD SPRING TWENTY FEET ACROSS SPACE AT THE DIZZY HEIGHTS OF THE FOREST TOP AND GRASP WITH UNERRING PRECISION A LIMB WAVING WILDLY IN THE PATH OF AN APPROACHING TORNADO.

HE COULD DROP TWENTY FEET AT A STRETCH FROM LIMB TO LIMB IN RAPID DESCENT TO THE GROUND...

...OR HE COULD GAIN THE UTMOST PINNACLE OF THE LOFTIEST TROPICAL GIANT WITH THE EASE AND SWIFTNESS OF A SQUIRREL. THOUGH BUT TEN YEARS OLD, HE WAS FULLY AS STRONG AS THE AVERAGE MAN OF THIRTY, AND FAR MORE AGILE THAN THE MOST PRACTICED ATHLETE EVER BECOMES. AND DAY BY DAY HIS STRENGTH WAS INCREASING. HIS LIFE AMONG THESE FIERCE APES WAS HAPPY; FOR HIS RECOLLECTION HELD NO OTHER LIFE...

...NOR DID HE KNOW THAT THERE EXISTED IN THE UNIVERSE AUGHT ELSE THAN HIS LITTLE FOREST AND THE WILD JUNGLE ANIMALS WITH WHICH HE WAS FAMILIAR.

HE WAS NEARLY TEN WHEN HE REALIZED THAT A GREAT DIFFERENCE EXISTED BETWEEN HIMSELF AND HIS FELLOWS. HIS LITTLE BODY, BURNED BROWN BY EXPOSURE, SUDDENLY CAUSED HIM FEELINGS OF INTENSE SHAME, FOR HE REALIZED THAT IT WAS ENTIRELY HAIRLESS, LIKE SOME LOW SNAKE OR OTHER REPTILE.

HE ATTEMPTED TO OBVIATE THIS BY PLASTERING HIMSELF FROM HEAD TO FOOT WITH MUD, BUT THIS DRIED AND FELL OFF. BESIDES, IT FELT SO UNCOMFORTABLE THAT HE QUICKLY DECIDED THAT HE PREFERRED THE SHAME TO THE DISCOMFORT.

IN THE HIGHER LAND WHICH HIS TRIBE FREQUENTED WAS A LITTLE LAKE, AND IT WAS HERE THAT TARZAN FIRST SAW HIS FACE IN THE CLEAR, STILL WATERS OF ITS BOSOM.

IT WAS ON A SULTRY DAY OF THE DRY SEASON THAT HE AND ONE OF HIS COUSINS HAD GONE DOWN TO THE BANK TO DRINK. AS THEY LEANED OVER, BOTH LITTLE FACES WERE MIRRORED ON THE PLACID POOL: THE FIERCE AND TERRIBLE FEATURES OF THE APE BESIDE THOSE OF THE ARISTOCRATIC SCION OF AN OLD ENGLISH HOUSE. TARZAN WAS APPALLED. IT HAD BEEN BAD ENOUGH TO BE HAIRLESS, BUT TO OWN SUCH A COUNTENANCE! HE WONDERED THAT THE OTHER APES COULD LOOK AT HIM AT ALL. THAT TINY SLIT OF A MOUTH AND THOSE PUNY WHITE TEETH! HOW THEY LOOKED BESIDE THE MIGHTY LIPS AND POWERFUL FANGS OF HIS MORE FORTUNATE BROTHERS! AND THE LITTLE PINCHED NOSE OF HIS; SO THIN WAS IT THAT IT LOOKED HALF STARVED.

HE TURNED RED AS HE COMPARED IT WITH THE BEAUTIFUL BROAD NOSTRILS OF HIS COMPANION. SUCH A GENEROUS NOSE! WHY IT SPREAD HALF ACROSS HIS FACE! IT CERTAINLY MUST BE FINE TO BE SO HANDSOME, THOUGHT POOR LITTLE TARZAN. BUT WHEN HE SAW HIS OWN EYES; AH, THAT WAS THE FINAL BLOW — A BROWN SPOT, A GRAY CIRCLE, AND THEN BLANK WHITENESS! FRIGHTFUL! NOT EVEN THE SNAKES HAD SUCH HIDEOUS EYES AS HE.

SO INTENT WAS HE
UPON THIS PERSONAL
APPRAISEMENT OF HIS
FEATURES THAT HE DID NOT
HEAR THE PARTING OF THE TALL
GRASS BEHIND HIM AS A GREAT
BODY PUSHED ITSELF STEALTHILY
THROUGH THE JUNGLE; NOR DID HIS
COMPANION, THE APE, HEAR EITHER, FOR
HE WAS DRINKING AND THE NOISE OF HIS
SUCKING LIPS AND GURGLES OF SATISFACTION
DROWNED THE QUIET APPROACH OF THE INTRUDER.

NOT THIRTY PACES BEHIND THE TWO SHE CROUCHED—
SABOR, THE LIONESS—LASHING HER TAIL. CAUTIOUSLY SHE
MOVED A GREAT PADDED PAW FORWARD, NOISELESSLY PLACING
IT BEFORE SHE LIFTED THE NEXT. THUS SHE ADVANCED, HER BELLY
LOW, ALMOST TOUCHING THE SURFACE OF THE GROUND—A
GREAT CAT PREPARING TO SPRING UPON ITS PREY.

NOW SHE WAS WITHIN TEN FEET OF THE TWO UNSUSPECTING LITTLE PLAYFELLOWS—CAREFULLY SHE DREW HER HIND FEET WELL UP BENEATH HER BODY, THE GREAT MUSCLES ROLLING UNDER THE BEAUTIFUL SKIN.

SO LOW WAS SHE CROUCHING NOW THAT SHE SEEMED FLATTENED TO THE EARTH EXCEPT FOR THE UPWARD BEND OF THE GLOSSY BACK AS IT GATHERED FOR THE SPRING.

NO LONGER THE TAIL LASHED—QUIET AND STRAIGHT BEHIND HER IT LAY. AN INSTANT SHE PAUSED THUS AS THOUGH TURNED TO STONE...

...AND THEN, WITH AN AWFUL SCREAM, SHE SPRANG.

HER SCREAM WAS NOT A WARNING. IT
PRODUCED A PARALYSIS OF TERROR AS
THE LITTLE APE CROUCHED AND FROZE—
AND THAT WAS HIS UNDOING. NOT SO, HOWEVER,
WITH TARZAN, THE MAN-CHILD. HIS LIFE AMIDST THE
DANGERS OF THE JUNGLE HAD TAUGHT HIM TO MEET
EMERGENCIES WITH SELF-CONFIDENCE, AND HIS
HIGHER INTELLIGENCE RESULTED IN A QUICKNESS OF
MENTAL ACTION FAR BEYOND THE POWERS OF THE APES.
THE CRY OF SABOR GALVANIZED HIM INTO INSTANT
ACTION. INTO THE DEEP WATERS OF THE LAKE HE PLUNGED...

...AN EVIL HARDLY LESS THAN SABOR'S FANGS—FOR HE COULD NOT SWIM. RAPIDLY HE MOVED HIS HANDS AND FEET. BY
CHANCE HE FELL INTO A STROKE A DOG USES. IN A FEW SECONDS HIS NOSE WAS ABOVE WATER.

THE LIONESS WAS INTENTLY WATCHING TARZAN, EVIDENTLY EXPECTING HIM TO RETURN TO SHORE, BUT THIS THE BOY HAD NO INTENTION OF DOING. INSTEAD HE RAISED HIS VOICE IN THE CALL OF DISTRESS COMMON TO HIS TRIBE.

ALMOST IMMEDIATELY FORTY OR MORE GREAT APES SWUNG TOWARD THE SCENE.

WITH A SNARL OF HATRED THE LIONESS VANISHED. TARZAN NOW SWAM TO SHORE EXHILARATED BY THE EXPERIENCE AND THE KNOWLEDGE OF HIS NEW-FOUND SKILL. AND EVER AFTER HE LOST NO OPPORTUNITY TO TAKE A DAILY PLUNGE IN LAKE OR STREAM OR OCEAN WHEN IT WAS POSSIBLE TO DO SO.

FOR A LONG TIME KALA COULD NOT ACCUSTOM HERSELF TO THE SIGHT; FOR THOUGH HER PEOPLE COULD SWIM WHEN FORCED TO IT, THEY DID NOT LIKE TO ENTER WATER, AND NEVER DID SO VOLUNTARILY.

THE ADVENTURE WITH THE LIONESS GAVE TARZAN FOOD FOR PLEASURABLE MEMORIES, FOR IT WAS SUCH AFFAIRS WHICH BROKE THE MONOTONY OF HIS DAILY LIFE — OTHERWISE BUT A DULL ROUND OF SEARCHING FOR FOOD, EATING, AND SLEEPING. THE TRIBE TO WHICH HE BELONGED ROAMED A TRACT EXTENDING, ROUGHLY, TWENTY-FIVE MILES ALONG THE SEACOAST AND SOME FIFTY MILES INLAND. THIS THEY TRAVERSED ALMOST CONTINUALLY, OCCASIONALLY REMAINING FOR MONTHS IN ONE LOCALITY; BUT AS THEY MOVED THROUGH THE TREES WITH GREAT SPEED, THEY OFTEN COVERED THE TERRITORY IN A VERY FEW DAYS.

MUCH DEPENDED UPON FOOD SUPPLY, CLIMATIC CONDITIONS, AND THE PREVALENCE OF ANIMALS OF THE MORE DANGEROUS SPECIES; THOUGH KERCHAK OFTEN LED THEM ON LONG MARCHES FOR NO OTHER REASON THAN THAT HE HAD TIRED OF REMAINING IN THE SAME PLACE.

AT NIGHT THEY SLEPT WHERE DARKNESS OVERTOOK THEM, LYING UPON THE GROUND, AND SOMETIMES COVERING THEIR HEADS, AND MORE SELDOM THEIR BODIES, WITH THE GREAT LEAVES OF THE ELEPHANT'S EAR. TWO OR THREE MIGHT LIE CUDDLED IN EACH OTHER'S ARMS FOR ADDITIONAL WARMTH IF THE NIGHT WERE CHILL, AND THUS TARZAN HAD SLEPT IN KALA'S ARMS NIGHTLY FOR ALL THESE YEARS.

THAT THE HUGE, FIERCE BRUTE LOVED THIS CHILD OF ANOTHER RACE IS BEYOND QUESTION, AND HE, TOO, GAVE TO THE GREAT, HAIRY BEAST ALL THE AFFECTION THAT WOULD HAVE BELONGED TO HIS FAIR YOUNG MOTHER HAD SHE LIVED. WHEN HE WAS DISOBEDIENT SHE CUFFED HIM, IT IS TRUE, BUT SHE WAS NEVER CRUEL TO HIM, AND WAS MORE OFTEN CARESSING HIM THAN CHASTISING HIM.

TUBLAT, HER HUSBAND, ALWAYS HATED TARZAN, AND ON SEVERAL OCCASIONS HAD COME NEAR ENDING HIS YOUTHFUL CAREER.

TARZAN ON HIS PART NEVER LOST AN OPPORTUNITY TO SHOW THAT HE FULLY RECIPROCATED HIS FOSTER FATHER'S SENTIMENTS, AND WHENEVER HE COULD SAFELY ANNOY HIM OR HURL INSULTS UPON HIM, HE DID SO.

HIS SUPERIOR INTELLIGENCE AND CUNNING PERMITTED HIM TO INVENT A THOUSAND DIABOLICAL TRICKS TO ADD TO THE BURDENS OF TUBLAT'S LIFE. EARLY IN HIS BOYHOOD, HE HAD LEARNED TO FORM ROPES BY TWISTING AND TYING LONG GRASSES TOGETHER, AND WITH THESE HE WAS FOREVER TRIPPING TUBLAT OR ATTEMPTING TO HANG HIM FROM SOME OVERHANGING BRANCH.

THE WANDERINGS OF THE TRIBE BROUGHT THEM OFTEN NEAR THE CLOSED AND SILENT CABIN . TO TARZAN THIS WAS A NEVER-ENDING SOURCE OF MYSTERY AND PLEASURE .

USUALLY HE WAS ALONE WHEN HE VISITED IT , FOR THE APES HAD NO LOVE FOR THE DESERTED ABODE. HE WOULD PEEK INTO THE WINDOWS OR CLIMB TO THE ROOF TO PEER DOWN THE CHIMNEY . BUT HE COULD FIND NO MEANS OF INGRESS .

THE STORY OF HIS OWN CONNECTION WITH THE CABIN HAD NEVER BEEN TOLD HIM. THE LANGUAGE OF THE APES HAS SO FEW WORDS THAT THEY COULD TALK BUT LITTLE OF WHAT THEY HAD SEEN IN THE CABIN. ONLY IN A DIM, VAGUE WAY HAD KALA EXPLAINED TO HIM THAT HIS FATHER HAD BEEN A STRANGE WHITE APE, BUT HE DID NOT KNOW THAT KALA WAS NOT HIS OWN MOTHER.

BUT ONE DAY TARZAN NOTICED THAT THE DOOR WAS AN INDEPENDENT PART OF THE WALL IN WHICH IT WAS SET, AND FOR THE FIRST TIME IT OCCURRED TO HIM THAT THIS MIGHT PROVE THE MEANS OF ENTRANCE WHICH HAD SO LONG ELUDED HIM.

ON THIS DAY, THEN, HE WENT DIRECTLY TO THE DOOR AND SPENT HOURS EXAMINING IT AND FUSSING WITH THE HINGES, THE KNOB, AND THE LATCH. FINALLY HE STUMBLED UPON THE RIGHT COMBINATION, AND THE DOOR SWUNG CREAKINGLY OPEN BEFORE HIS ASTONISHED EYES.

ON THE FLOOR LAY A SKELETON, ON THE BED ANOTHER — AND A THIRD, A WEE MITE IN A CRADLE. THAT THESE WERE EVIDENCES OF A FEARFUL TRAGEDY OF A LONG DEAD DAY. HE GAVE NO HEED, NOR HAD HE ANY IDEA THESE WERE THE REMAINS OF HIS OWN FATHER AND MOTHER.

THE OTHER CONTENTS OF THE ROOM CLAIMED HIS ATTENTION — TOOLS, WEAPONS, BOOKS, CLOTHING. HE OPENED CHESTS AND CUPBOARDS.

HE CAME UPON A SHARP HUNTING KNIFE, AND PROMPTLY CUT HIS FINGER.

UNDAUNTED, HE AMUSED HIMSELF WITH HIS NEW TOY, HACKING SPLINTERS FROM THE TABLE AND CHAIRS.

IN A CUPBOARD FILLED WITH BOOKS HE CAME ACROSS ONE WITH BRIGHTLY COLORED PICTURES — IT WAS A CHILD'S ILLUSTRATED ALPHABET — A IS FOR ARCHER B IS FOR BOY

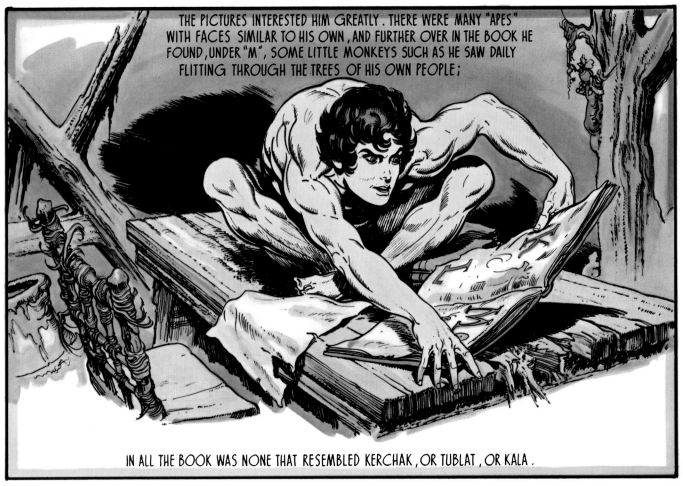

THE PICTURES INTERESTED HIM GREATLY. THERE WERE MANY "APES" WITH FACES SIMILAR TO HIS OWN, AND FURTHER OVER IN THE BOOK HE FOUND, UNDER "M", SOME LITTLE MONKEYS SUCH AS HE SAW DAILY FLITTING THROUGH THE TREES OF HIS OWN PEOPLE;

IN ALL THE BOOK WAS NONE THAT RESEMBLED KERCHAK, OR TUBLAT, OR KALA.

AT FIRST HE TRIED TO PICK THE LITTLE FIGURES FROM THE LEAVES, BUT HE SOON SAW THAT THEY WERE NOT REAL, THOUGH HE KNEW NOT WHAT THEY MIGHT BE, NOR HAD HE ANY WORDS TO DESCRIBE THEM. THE BOATS, AND TRAINS, AND COWS, AND HORSES WERE QUITE MEANINGLESS TO HIM, BUT NOT QUITE SO BAFFLING AS THE ODD LITTLE FIGURES WHICH APPEARED BENEATH AND BETWEEN THE COLORED PICTURES — SOME STRANGE KIND OF BUG HE THOUGHT THEY MIGHT BE, FOR MANY OF THEM HAD LEGS, THOUGH NOWHERE COULD HE FIND ONE WITH EYES AND A MOUTH.

IT WAS HIS FIRST INTRODUCTION TO THE LETTERS OF THE ALPHABET, AND HE WAS OVER TEN YEARS OLD. OF COURSE HE HAD NEVER BEFORE SEEN PRINT, NEVER HAD SPOKEN WITH ANY LIVING THING WHICH HAD THE REMOTEST IDEA THAT SUCH A THING AS A WRITTEN LANGUAGE EXISTED, NOR EVER HAD HE SEEN ANYONE READING. SO WHAT WONDER THAT THE LITTLE BOY WAS QUITE AT A LOSS TO GUESS THE MEANING OF THESE STRANGE FIGURES. NEAR THE MIDDLE OF THE BOOK HE FOUND HIS OLD ENEMY, SABOR, THE LIONESS, AND FURTHER ON, COILED HISTAH, THE SNAKE.

OH, IT WAS MOST ENGROSSING! NEVER BEFORE IN ALL HIS TEN YEARS HAD HE ENJOYED ANYTHING SO MUCH. SO ABSORBED WAS HE THAT HE DID NOT NOTE THE APPROACHING DUSK, UNTIL IT WAS QUITE UPON HIM AND THE FIGURES WERE BLURRED.

HE PUT THE BOOK BACK IN THE CUPBOARD AND CLOSED THE DOOR, FOR HE DID NOT WISH ANYONE ELSE TO FIND AND DESTROY HIS TREASURE, AND AS HE WENT OUT INTO THE GATHERING DARKNESS HE CLOSED THE GREAT DOOR OF THE CABIN BEHIND HIM AS IT HAD BEEN BEFORE HE DISCOVERED THE SECRET OF ITS LOCK. BUT BEFORE HE LEFT, HE HAD NOTICED THE HUNTING KNIFE LYING WHERE HE HAD THROWN IT UPON THE FLOOR, AND THIS HE PICKED UP AND TOOK WITH HIM TO SHOW TO HIS FELLOWS.

HE HAD TAKEN SCARCE A DOZEN STEPS TOWARD THE JUNGLE WHEN A GREAT FORM ROSE UP BEFORE HIM FROM THE SHADOWS OF A LOW BUSH. AT FIRST HE THOUGHT IT WAS ONE OF HIS OWN PEOPLE, BUT IN ANOTHER INSTANT HE REALIZED THAT IT WAS BOLGANI, THE HUGE GORILLA.

SO CLOSE WAS HE THAT THERE WAS NO CHANCE FOR FLIGHT AND LITTLE TARZAN KNEW THAT HE MUST STAND AND FIGHT FOR HIS LIFE, FOR THESE GREAT BEASTS WERE THE DEADLY ENEMIES OF HIS TRIBE, AND NEITHER ONE NOR THE OTHER EVER ASKED OR GAVE QUARTER.

HE WAS A BOY, BUT HE MET THE GORILLA WITHOUT A TRACE OF TREMOR OR PANIC. HE STRUCK THE CHARGING BRUTE WITH CLOSED FISTS. BUT IN ONE HAND HE CLUTCHED THE KNIFE. AS THE BRUTE LUNGED, ACCIDENTALLY THE KNIFE SANK DEEP INTO THE HAIRY BREAST.

BUT THE BOY HAD LEARNED IN THAT BRIEF SECOND A USE FOR HIS SHARP AND SHINING TOY, SO THAT, AS THE TEARING, STRIKING BEAST DRAGGED HIM TO THE EARTH, HE PLUNGED THE BLADE REPEATEDLY AND TO THE HILT INTO ITS BREAST.

THE GORILLA, FIGHTING AFTER THE MANNER OF ITS KIND, STRUCK TERRIFIC BLOWS WITH ITS OPEN HAND AND TORE THE FLESH AT THE BOY'S THROAT AND CHEST WITH ITS MIGHTY TUSKS.

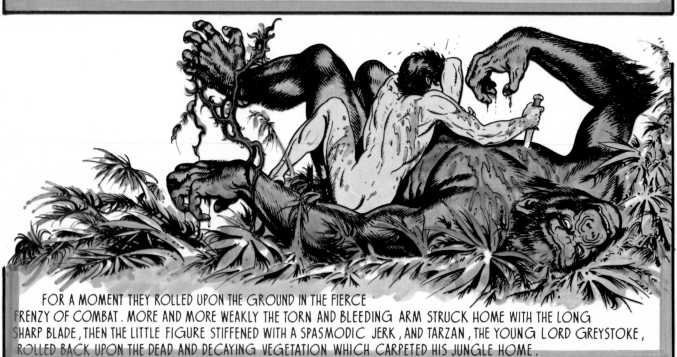

FOR A MOMENT THEY ROLLED UPON THE GROUND IN THE FIERCE FRENZY OF COMBAT. MORE AND MORE WEAKLY THE TORN AND BLEEDING ARM STRUCK HOME WITH THE LONG SHARP BLADE, THEN THE LITTLE FIGURE STIFFENED WITH A SPASMODIC JERK, AND TARZAN, THE YOUNG LORD GREYSTOKE, ROLLED BACK UPON THE DEAD AND DECAYING VEGETATION WHICH CARPETED HIS JUNGLE HOME.

BACK IN THE FOREST THE TRIBE HAD HEARD THE FIERCE CHALLENGE OF THE GORILLA. AND KALA, SEEING THAT TARZAN WAS MISSING, FAIRLY FLEW THROUGH THE TREES. DARKNESS HAD NOW FALLEN, AND AN EARLY MOON WAS SENDING ITS FAINT LIGHT TO CAST STRANGE, GROTESQUE SHADOWS AMONG THE DENSE FOLIAGE OF THE FOREST.

LIKE SOME HUGE PHANTOM, KALA SWUNG NOISELESSLY FROM TREE TO TREE; NOW RUNNING NIMBLY ALONG A GREAT BRANCH, NOW SWINGING THROUGH SPACE AT THE END OF ANOTHER, IN HER RAPID PROGRESS. THAT HER LITTLE TARZAN COULD DESTROY A GREAT BULL GORILLA SHE KNEW TO BE IMPROBABLE, AND SO, AS SHE NEARED THE SPOT FROM WHICH THE SOUNDS OF THE STRUGGLE HAD COME, SHE MOVED WITH EXTREME CAUTION AS SHE TRAVERSED THE LOWEST BRANCHES, PEERING EAGERLY INTO THE MOON-SPLASHED BLACKNESS FOR A SIGN OF THE COMBATANTS.

PRESENTLY SHE CAME UPON THEM, LYING IN A LITTLE OPEN SPACE FULL UNDER THE BRILLIANT LIGHT OF THE MOON — LITTLE TARZAN'S TORN AND BLOODY FORM, AND BESIDE IT A GREAT BULL GORILLA, STONE DEAD.

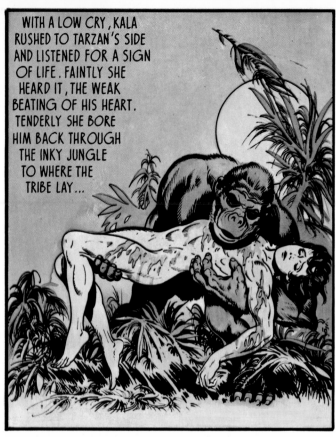

WITH A LOW CRY, KALA RUSHED TO TARZAN'S SIDE AND LISTENED FOR A SIGN OF LIFE. FAINTLY SHE HEARD IT, THE WEAK BEATING OF HIS HEART. TENDERLY SHE BORE HIM BACK THROUGH THE INKY JUNGLE TO WHERE THE TRIBE LAY...

...AND FOR MANY DAYS AND NIGHTS SHE SAT GUARD BESIDE HIM, BRINGING HIM FOOD AND WATER, AND BRUSHING THE FLIES AND OTHER INSECTS FROM HIS CRUEL WOUNDS.

OF MEDICINE OR SURGERY THE
POOR THING KNEW NOTHING. SHE
COULD BUT LICK THE WOUNDS, AND THUS
SHE KEPT THEM CLEANSED, THAT HEALING
NATURE MIGHT THE MORE QUICKLY DO
HER WORK. AT FIRST TARZAN WOULD EAT
NOTHING, BUT ROLLED AND TOSSED IN A
WILD DELIRIUM OF FEVER. ALL HE CRAVED
WAS WATER, AND THIS SHE BROUGHT HIM IN
THE ONLY WAY SHE COULD, BEARING IT IN HER OWN MOUTH.
    NO HUMAN MOTHER COULD HAVE SHOWN MORE UNSELFISH
AND SACRIFICING DEVOTION THAN DID THIS POOR, WILD BRUTE
FOR THE LITTLE ORPHANED WAIF WHOM FATE HAD THROWN INTO HER KEEPING.
    AT LAST THE FEVER ABATED AND THE BOY COMMENCED TO MEND. NO WORD OF
COMPLAINT PASSED HIS TIGHT SET LIPS, THOUGH THE PAIN OF HIS WOUNDS WAS
EXCRUCIATING. WITH THE STOICISM OF THE BRUTES WHO HAD RAISED HIM, HE
ENDURED HIS SUFFERING QUIETLY, PREFERRING TO CRAWL AWAY FROM THE OTHERS
AND LIE HUDDLED IN SOME CLUMP OF TALL GRASSES RATHER THAN TO SHOW HIS
MISERY BEFORE THEIR EYES. KALA, ALONE, HE WAS GLAD TO HAVE WITH HIM, BUT
NOW THAT HE WAS BETTER SHE WAS GONE LONGER AT A TIME, IN SEARCH OF
FOOD; FOR THE DEVOTED ANIMAL HAD SCARCELY EATEN ENOUGH TO SUPPORT
HER OWN LIFE WHILE TARZAN HAD BEEN SO LOW, AND SHE WAS, IN CONSEQUENCE,
REDUCED TO A MERE SHADOW OF HER FORMER SELF.
    AFTER WHAT SEEMED AN ETERNITY TO THE LITTLE
SUFFERER, HE WAS ABLE TO WALK ONCE MORE, AND
FROM THEN ON HIS RECOVERY WAS RAPID, SO THAT
IN ANOTHER MONTH HE WAS AS STRONG AND ACTIVE
AS EVER. DURING HIS CONVALESCENCE, HE HAD GONE
OVER IN HIS MIND MANY TIMES THE BATTLE WITH THE
GORILLA, AND HIS FIRST THOUGHT WAS TO RECOVER
THE WONDERFUL LITTLE WEAPON WHICH HAD TRANSFORMED
HIM FROM A HOPELESSLY OUTCLASSED WEAKLING
TO THE SUPERIOR OF THE MIGHTY TERROR OF
THE JUNGLE.
    THUS DID TARZAN END THE FIRST, CURIOUS
CHAPTER OF HIS YOUNG LIFE. AN EVEN STRANGER
ONE WAS TO FOLLOW.

BOOK TWO

OF THE APES

AFTER A SEARCH NEAR THE BONES OF HIS GREAT ADVERSARY HE FOUND THE FORMIDABLE KNIFE NOW RED WITH RUST.

NOW, FULLY RECOVERED FROM HIS BATTLE WITH BOLGANI THE GORILLA, TARZAN BECAME ANXIOUS TO RETURN TO THE CABIN WITH ITS WONDROUS CONTENTS. ONE MORNING HE SET FORTH ON HIS QUEST.

IN ANOTHER MOMENT HE WAS AT THE CABIN, AND HAD THROWN THE LATCH AND ENTERED. HIS FIRST CONCERN WAS TO LEARN THE MECHANISM OF THE LOCK SO THAT HE COULD LEARN PRECISELY WHAT CAUSED IT TO HOLD THE DOOR. HE FOUND THAT HE COULD CLOSE AND LOCK THE DOOR FROM WITHIN, AND THIS HE DID SO THAT THERE WOULD BE NO CHANCE OF HIS BEING MOLESTED WHILE AT HIS INVESTIGATIONS.

HE COMMENCED A SYSTEMATIC SEARCH OF THE CABIN; BUT HIS ATTENTION WAS SOON RIVETED BY THE BOOKS ...

... WHICH SEEMED TO EXERT A STRANGE AND POWERFUL INFLUENCE OVER HIM.

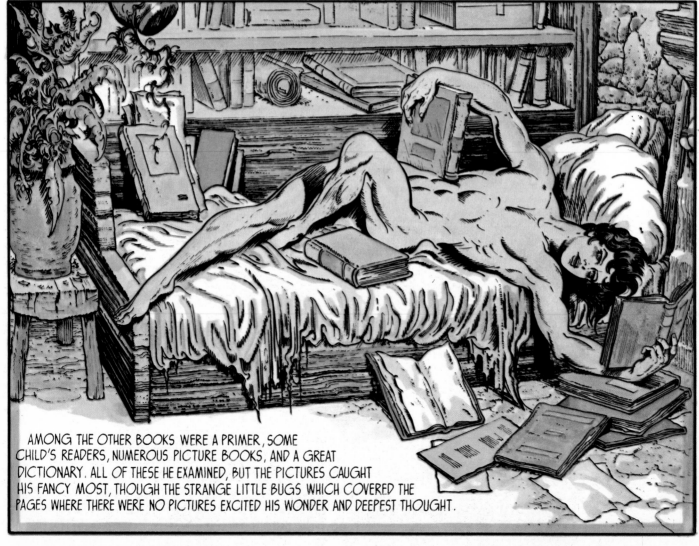

AMONG THE OTHER BOOKS WERE A PRIMER, SOME CHILD'S READERS, NUMEROUS PICTURE BOOKS, AND A GREAT DICTIONARY. ALL OF THESE HE EXAMINED, BUT THE PICTURES CAUGHT HIS FANCY MOST, THOUGH THE STRANGE LITTLE BUGS WHICH COVERED THE PAGES WHERE THERE WERE NO PICTURES EXCITED HIS WONDER AND DEEPEST THOUGHT.

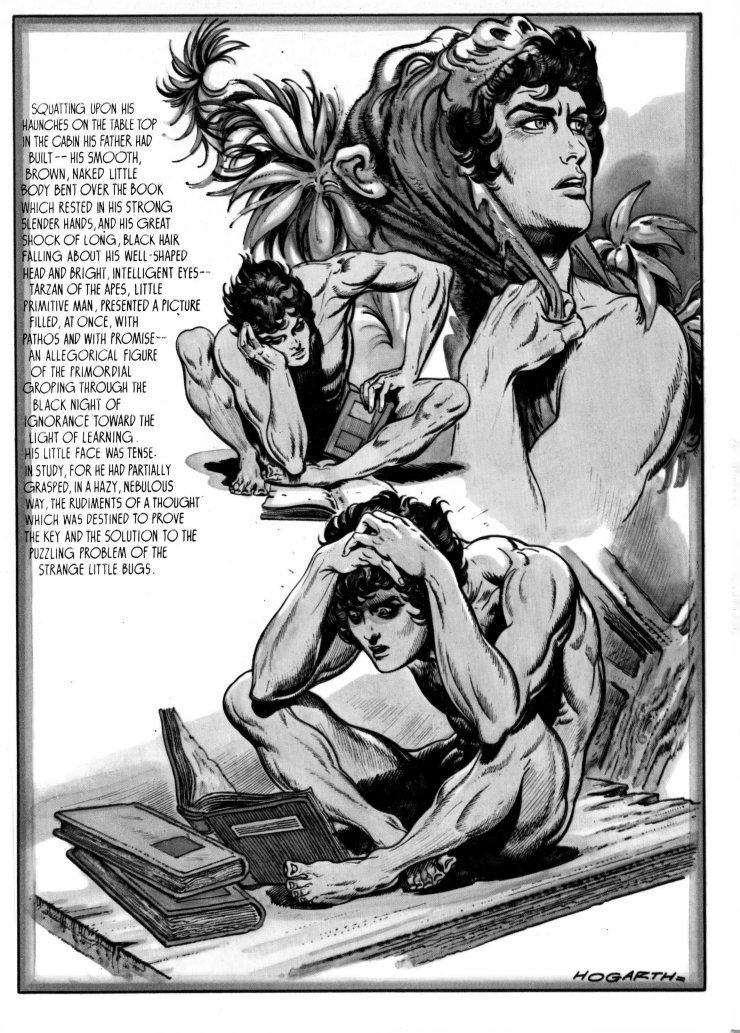

SQUATTING UPON HIS
HAUNCHES ON THE TABLE TOP
IN THE CABIN HIS FATHER HAD
BUILT -- HIS SMOOTH,
BROWN, NAKED LITTLE
BODY BENT OVER THE BOOK
WHICH RESTED IN HIS STRONG
SLENDER HANDS, AND HIS GREAT
SHOCK OF LONG, BLACK HAIR
FALLING ABOUT HIS WELL-SHAPED
HEAD AND BRIGHT, INTELLIGENT EYES--
TARZAN OF THE APES, LITTLE
PRIMITIVE MAN, PRESENTED A PICTURE
FILLED, AT ONCE, WITH
PATHOS AND WITH PROMISE--
AN ALLEGORICAL FIGURE
OF THE PRIMORDIAL
GROPING THROUGH THE
BLACK NIGHT OF
IGNORANCE TOWARD THE
LIGHT OF LEARNING.
HIS LITTLE FACE WAS TENSE
IN STUDY, FOR HE HAD PARTIALLY
GRASPED, IN A HAZY, NEBULOUS
WAY, THE RUDIMENTS OF A THOUGHT
WHICH WAS DESTINED TO PROVE
THE KEY AND THE SOLUTION TO THE
PUZZLING PROBLEM OF THE
STRANGE LITTLE BUGS.

HOGARTH=

IN HIS HANDS WAS A PRIMER OPENED AT A PICTURE OF A LITTLE APE SIMILAR TO HIMSELF, BUT COVERED, EXCEPT FOR HANDS AND FACE, WITH STRANGE, COLORED FUR, FOR SUCH HE THOUGHT THE JACKET AND TROUSERS TO BE. BENEATH THE PICTURE WERE THREE LITTLE BUGS -- B O Y.

AND NOW HE HAD DISCOVERED IN THE TEXT UPON THE PAGE THAT THESE THREE WERE REPEATED MANY TIMES IN THE SAME SEQUENCE. ANOTHER FACT HE LEARNED -- THAT THERE WERE COMPARATIVELY FEW INDIVIDUAL BUGS; BUT THESE WERE REPEATED MANY TIMES, OCCASIONALLY ALONE, BUT MORE OFTEN IN COMPANY WITH OTHERS.

SLOWLY HE TURNED THE PAGES, SCANNING THE PICTURES AND THE TEXT FOR A REPETITION OF THE COMBINATION B-O-Y. PRESENTLY HE FOUND IT BENEATH A PICTURE OF ANOTHER LITTLE APE AND A STRANGE ANIMAL WHICH WENT UPON FOUR LEGS LIKE THE JACKAL AND RESEMBLED HIM NOT A LITTLE. BENEATH THIS PICTURE THE BUGS APPEARED AS: A BOY AND A DOG.

THERE THEY WERE, THE THREE LITTLE BUGS WHICH ALWAYS ACCOMPANIED THE LITTLE APE.

AND SO HE PROGRESSED VERY, VERY SLOWLY, FOR IT WAS A HARD AND LABORIOUS TASK WHICH HE HAD SET HIMSELF WITHOUT KNOWING IT -- A TASK WHICH MIGHT SEEM TO YOU OR ME IMPOSSIBLE -- LEARNING TO READ WITHOUT HAVING THE SLIGHTEST KNOWLEDGE OF LETTERS OR WRITTEN LANGUAGE, OR THE FAINTEST IDEA THAT SUCH THINGS EXISTED.

HE DID NOT ACCOMPLISH IT IN A DAY, OR IN A WEEK, OR IN A MONTH, OR IN A YEAR; BUT SLOWLY, VERY SLOWLY, HE LEARNED AFTER HE HAD GRASPED THE POSSIBILITIES WHICH LAY IN THOSE LITTLE BUGS ...

... SO THAT BY THE TIME HE WAS FIFTEEN HE KNEW THE VARIOUS COMBINATIONS OF LETTERS WHICH STOOD FOR EVERY PRINTED FIGURE IN THE LITTLE PRIMER AND IN ONE OR TWO OF THE PICTURE BOOKS.

HOGARTH.

ONE DAY WHEN HE WAS ABOUT TWELVE, HE FOUND A NUMBER OF LEAD PENCILS, AND HE WAS DELIGHTED TO DISCOVER THE BLACK LINE ONE OF THEM LEFT WHEN IT WAS SCRATCHED ON THE TABLE TOP.

SOON, AFTER A MASS OF SCRAWLY LOOPS, HE ATTEMPTED TO REPRODUCE THE BUGS HE SAW IN HIS BOOKS. IT WAS A DIFFICULT TASK, BUT HE HAD MADE A BEGINNING AT WRITING.

HE PERSEVERED FOR MONTHS. AND BY THE TIME HE WAS SEVENTEEN, HE HAD LEARNED THE WONDERFUL PURPOSE OF THE BOOKS WITH THE BUGS.

NO LONGER DID HE FEEL SHAME FOR HIS HAIRLESS BODY OR HIS HUMAN FEATURES, FOR NOW HIS REASON TOLD HIM THAT HE WAS OF A DIFFERENT RACE FROM HIS WILD AND HAIRY COMPANIONS. HE WAS A M-A-N, THEY WERE A-P-E-S, AND THE LITTLE APES WHICH SCURRIED THROUGH THE FOREST TOP WERE M-O-N-K-E-Y-S.

HE KNEW, TOO, THAT OLD SABOR WAS A L-I-O-N-E-S-S, AND HISTAH A S-N-A-K-E, AND TANTOR AN E-L-E-P-H-A-N-T. AND SO HE LEARNED TO READ.

THERE WERE MANY BREAKS IN HIS EDUCATION, CAUSED BY THE MIGRATORY HABITS OF HIS TRIBE, BUT EVEN WHEN REMOVED FROM RECOURSE TO HIS BOOKS, HIS ACTIVE BRAIN CONTINUED TO SEARCH OUT THE MYSTERIES OF THE FASCINATING BUGS.

PIECES OF BARK AND FLAT LEAVES AND EVEN SMOOTH STRETCHES OF BARE EARTH PROVIDED HIM WITH COPY BOOKS WHEREON TO SCRATCH WITH THE POINT OF HIS HUNTING KNIFE THE LESSONS HE WAS LEARNING. NOR DID HE NEGLECT THE STERNER DUTIES OF LIFE WHILE FOLLOWING THE BENT OF HIS INCLINATION TOWARD THE SOLVING OF THE MYSTERY OF HIS LIBRARY.

HE PRACTICED WITH HIS ROPE AND PLAYED WITH HIS SHARP KNIFE, WHICH HE HAD LEARNED TO KEEP KEEN BY WHETTING UPON FLAT STONES.

THE TRIBE HAD GROWN LARGER SINCE TARZAN HAD COME AMONG THEM, FOR UNDER THE LEADERSHIP OF KERCHAK THEY HAD PLENTY TO EAT AND LITTLE OR NO LOSS FROM PREDATORY INCURSIONS OF NEIGHBORS. THE YOUNGER MALES AS THEY BECAME ADULT FOUND IT MORE COMFORTABLE TO LIVE IN AMITY WITH KERCHAK RATHER THAN ATTEMPT TO SET UP A NEW ESTABLISHMENT OF THEIR OWN OR FIGHT WITH THE REDOUBTABLE BULL FOR SUPREMACY AT HOME. OCCASIONALLY ONE MORE FEROCIOUS THAN HIS FELLOWS WOULD ATTEMPT THIS LATTER ALTERNATIVE, BUT NONE HAD COME YET WHO COULD WREST THE PALM OF VICTORY FROM THE FIERCE AND BRUTAL APE.

TARZAN NOW HELD A PECULIAR POSITION IN THE TRIBE, BUT ONE DAY TARZAN AT LAST ESTABLISHED HIS RIGHT TO RESPECT. THE TRIBE WAS GATHERED ABOUT A SMALL NATURAL AMPHITHEATER IN WHOSE CENTER WAS A STRANGE EARTHEN DRUM.

HERE THE TRIBE PERFORMED THE RITUAL OF THE DUM-DUM -- AND TODAY IT MARKED THE KILLING OF A GIANT APE, A MEMBER OF ANOTHER TRIBE.
MANY TRAVELERS HAVE SEEN THE DRUMS OF THE GREAT APES, AND SOME HAVE HEARD THE SOUNDS OF THEIR BEATING AND THE NOISE OF THE WILD, WEIRD REVELRY OF THESE FIRST LORDS OF THE JUNGLE, BUT TARZAN, LORD GREYSTOKE, IS, DOUBTLESS, THE ONLY HUMAN BEING WHO EVER JOINED IN THE FIERCE, MAD, INTOXICATING REVEL OF THE DUM-DUM.

CEREMONIOUSLY, THE PEOPLE OF KERCHAK LAID THEIR BURDEN BEFORE THE EARTHEN DRUM, AND SQUATTED BESIDE IT AS GUARDS. FOR A TIME ABSOLUTE QUIET REIGNED IN THE CLEARING--

--UNTIL THE RISING MOON GAVE THE SIGNAL FOR THE SAVAGE ORGY. NOW THREE OLD FEMALES BEGAN TAPPING ON THE RESOUNDING SURFACE OF THE DRUM, EACH WITH A KNOTTED BRANCH.

THE GREAT CIRCLE OF APES MOVED TO THE RHYTHMIC DIN AND FREQUENCY OF THEIR BLOWS, UNTIL THE JUNGLE ECHOED IN EVERY DIRECTION.

HUGE, FIERCE BRUTES STOPPED IN THEIR HUNTING, WITH UPPRICKED EARS AND RAISED HEADS, TO LISTEN TO THE DULL BOOMING THAT BETOKENED THE DUM-DUM OF THE APES.

THE GREAT CIRCLE
MOVED IN THE MAD WHIRL
OF THE DUM-DUM DANCE OF
DEATH. TARZAN, SWEAT-STREAKED
AND GLISTENING IN THE MOONLIGHT,
BECAME ONE WITH THE WILD,
LEAPING HORDE.

AT A SIGN FROM KERCHAK, THE DRUMS CEASED. THEN AS ONE, THE MALES RUSHED HEADLONG UPON THE DEAD
APE AND WITH BLOWS REDUCED IT TO A HAIRY PULP. GREAT FANGS SANK INTO THE
CARCASS, THE MIGHTIEST OF THE APES SEIZING THE CHOICEST MORSELS.

TARZAN WORMED INTO THE STRUGGLING MASS OF APES, AND WITH
HIS KNIFE SLASHED OFF A PORTION MORE THAN HE HAD HOPED FOR.

BUT OLD TUBLAT, KALA'S MATE AND TARZAN'S ENEMY, SPIED THE BOY CLUTCHING HIS PRIZE. WITH A WICKED GLEAM OF HATE HE MADE FOR HIM.

BUT TARZAN LEAPED NIMBLY AWAY, WITH HIS ARCH ENEMY CLOSE UPON HIS HEELS.

SWIFTLY HE SPED TOWARD THE SURROUNDING TREES, SPRANG TO A LOWER LIMB --

--AND CLIMBED RAPIDLY UPWARD TO THE WAVING PINNACLE OF A LOFTY GIANT. THE HEAVY TUBLAT DARED NOT FOLLOW. THERE TARZAN PERCHED, HURLING INSULTS AT THE RAGING BRUTE BELOW.

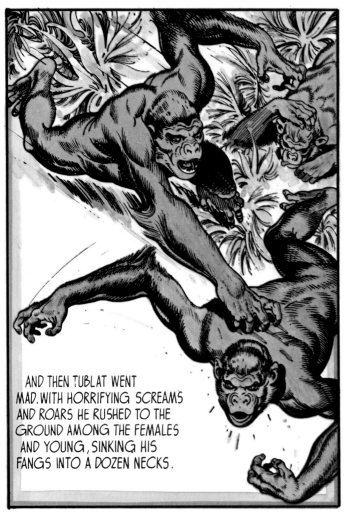

AND THEN TUBLAT WENT MAD. WITH HORRIFYING SCREAMS AND ROARS HE RUSHED TO THE GROUND AMONG THE FEMALES AND YOUNG, SINKING HIS FANGS INTO A DOZEN NECKS.

FROM ABOVE TARZAN WITNESSED THE MAD CARNIVAL OF RAGE. THEN TUBLAT SPIED A FEMALE MAKING FOR THE TREE WHERE TARZAN PERCHED. IT WAS KALA.

CLOSE BEHIND HER CAME THE AWFUL TUBLAT. AND AS QUICKLY TARZAN DROPPED LIKE A STONE TOWARD HIS FOSTER MOTHER.

WITH A ROAR TUBLAT LEAPED AS KALA SPRANG FOR AN OVERHANGING LIMB ALMOST ABOVE HIS HEAD. AND SHE WOULD HAVE BEEN SAFE--

--BUT THERE WAS A SUDDEN, TEARING SOUND. THE BRANCH BROKE, AND DOWN SHE CAME ON THE HEAD OF TUBLAT, KNOCKING HIM TO THE GROUND.

IN THAT INSTANT THE MAN-CHILD PLUNGED BETWEEN HIS FOSTER MOTHER AND THE INFURIATED BULL. NOTHING COULD HAVE SUITED THE FIERCE BEAST BETTER.

ONE BY ONE THE TRIBE SWUNG DOWN FROM THEIR ARBOREAL RETREATS AND FORMED A CIRCLE ABOUT TARZAN AND HIS VANQUISHED FOE. WHEN THEY HAD ALL COME TARZAN TURNED TOWARD THEM. "I AM TARZAN," HE CRIED. "I AM A GREAT KILLER. LET ALL RESPECT TARZAN OF THE APES AND KALA, HIS MOTHER."

"THERE BE NONE AMONG YOU AS MIGHTY AS TARZAN. LET HIS ENEMIES BEWARE." LOOKING FULL INTO THE WICKED, RED EYES OF KERCHAK, THE YOUNG LORD GREYSTOKE BEAT UPON HIS MIGHTY BREAST AND SCREAMED OUT ONCE MORE HIS SHRILL CRY OF DEFIANCE.

THE MORNING AFTER THE DUM-DUM THE TRIBE STARTED SLOWLY BACK THROUGH THE FOREST.

THE MARCH WAS A LEISURELY SEARCH FOR FOOD. ONCE OLD SABOR CROSSED THEIR PATH, AND THEY MOVED TO THE SAFETY OF THE HIGHER BRANCHES.

UPON A LOW-HANGING BRANCH SAT TARZAN. HE HURLED A PINEAPPLE, TAUNTING THE ANCIENT ENEMY OF HIS PEOPLE. WITH A LASH OF HER TAIL SHE BARED HER FANGS IN A HIDEOUS SNARL.

FOR A MOMENT THE TWO EYED EACH OTHER IN FIERCE CHALLENGE. IN TARZAN'S MIND A GREAT PLAN HAD SPRUNG. HE HAD KILLED MIGHTY TUBLAT; NOW HE WOULD TRACK DOWN THE CRAFTY SABOR AND SLAY HER LIKEWISE.

ABOVE EVERYTHING HE DESIRED SABOR'S SKIN TO COVER HIS NAKEDNESS WITH *CLOTHES*. HE HAD LEARNED FROM HIS PICTURE BOOKS THAT ALL *MEN* WERE SO COVERED.

DAYS AFTER HE HAD THOUGHT OF LITTLE ELSE.

ON THIS DAY, MORE IMMEDIATE INTERESTS WERE TO ATTRACT HIS ATTENTION. OF A SUDDEN IT BECAME AS MIDNIGHT; THE NOISES OF THE JUNGLE CEASED; THE TREES STOOD MOTIONLESS AS THOUGH IN PARALYZED EXPECTANCY OF SOME IMMINENT DANGER. ALL NATURE WAITED...

...BUT NOT FOR LONG. SUDDENLY, WITH AN AWESOME MOANING OF THE WIND, A VIVID AND BLINDING LIGHT AND A CANNONADE OF ROARING THUNDER, A STORM BROKE. THE TREES BENT, THEIR MIGHTY TOPS LASHING, AS THE DELUGE FELL UPON THE JUNGLE. FOR HOURS IT RAGED, WHILE THE TRIBE HUDDLED IN MISERY, SHIVERING FROM RAIN, COLD AND FEAR.

THE END WAS AS SUDDEN AS THE BEGINNING. THE WIND
CEASED, THE SUN SHONE FORTH--NATURE SMILED ONCE MORE.
THE DRIPPING LEAVES AND THE MOIST PETALS OF FLOWERS GLISTENED
IN THE SPLENDOR OF THE RETURNING DAY. NATURE FORGOT, HER CHILDREN
FORGOT, ALSO. BUSY LIFE WENT ON AS IT HAD BEEN BEFORE THE DARKNESS AND FRIGHT

BUT TO TARZAN A DAWNING LIGHT HAD COME TO EXPLAIN THE MYSTERY ABOUT
CLOTHES. HOW SNUG HE WOULD HAVE BEEN UNDER THE HEAVY COAT OF
SABOR! AND SO WAS ADDED A FURTHER INCENTIVE TO THE ADVENTURE.

ALWAYS WHEN JOURNEYING, TARZAN HAD KEPT HIS ROPE IN READINESS, PRACTISING WITH THE QUICK THROWN NOOSE.

ONCE HE SNARED HORTA, THE BOAR...

... AND ITS MAD LUNGE TOPPLED TARZAN FROM HIS PERCH. HE LOST A ROPE ON THIS OCCASION, BUT HAD IT BEEN SABOR WHO DRAGGED HIM DOWN, DOUBTLESS HE WOULD HAVE LOST HIS LIFE.

THUS BY EXPERIENCE HE LEARNED THE LIMITATIONS AS WELL AS THE POSSIBILITIES OF HIS STRANGE NEW WEAPON. IT TOOK HIM MANY DAYS TO BRAID A NEW ROPE, BUT WHEN IT WAS DONE, HE WENT FORTH PURPOSELY TO HUNT...

... TO LIE IN WAIT IN THE FOLIAGE OF A GREAT BRANCH ABOVE THE TRAIL THAT LED TO WATER.

SEVERAL SMALL ANIMALS PASSED UNHARMED BENEATH HIM. HE DID NOT WANT SUCH INSIGNIFICANT GAME. IT WOULD TAKE A STRONG ANIMAL TO TEST THE EFFICACY OF HIS NEW SCHEME.

AT LAST CAME SHE WHOM TARZAN SOUGHT, WITH SINEWS ROLLING BENEATH SHIMMERING HIDE; FAT AND GLOSSY CAME SABOR, THE LIONESS.

HER GREAT PADDED FEET FELL SOFT AND NOISELESS ON THE NARROW TRAIL. HER HEAD WAS HIGH IN EVER ALERT ATTENTION; HER LONG TAIL MOVED SLOWLY IN SINUOUS AND GRACEFUL UNDULATIONS. NEARER AND NEARER SHE CAME TO WHERE TARZAN OF THE APES CROUCHED UPON HIS LIMB, THE COILS OF HIS LONG ROPE POISED READY IN HIS HAND.

LIKE A THING OF BRONZE, MOTIONLESS AS DEATH, SAT TARZAN AS SABOR PASSED BENEATH.

THEN THE SILENT COIL SHOT OUT LIKE A GREAT SNAKE, LOOPED THE GLOSSY THROAT, AND WITH A JERK TARZAN DREW THE NOOSE TIGHT. SABOR WAS TRAPPED.

WITH A BOUND THE STARTLED BEAST TURNED INTO THE JUNGLE, BUT TARZAN WAS NOT TO LOSE ANOTHER ROPE THROUGH THE SAME CAUSE AS THE FIRST. THE LIONESS HAD TAKEN BUT HALF HER SECOND BOUND WHEN SHE FELT THE ROPE TIGHTEN ; HER BODY TURNED COMPLETELY OVER IN THE AIR AND SHE FELL WITH A CRASH UPON HER BACK. TARZAN HAD FASTENED THE END OF THE ROPE TO THE TRUNK OF THE GREAT TREE ON WHICH HE SAT.

BUT SABOR NOW FOUND IT WAS ONLY A SLENDER CORD THAT HELD HER, AND GRASPING IT IN HER JAWS SHE SEVERED IT, AND WAS FREE.

TARZAN MOCKED AND TAUNTED THE PACING, ROARING CREATURE, BUT HE WAS MUCH CHAGRINED. THE WELL-LAID PLAN HAD COME TO NAUGHT.

AT LAST, WITH A PARTING CHALLENGE AND A WELL-AIMED RIPE FRUIT INTO THE FACE OF HIS ADVERSARY, HE SWUNG AWAY TOWARD THE MEMBERS OF HIS TRIBE. IT WAS NOT THE LAST ENCOUNTER WITH SABOR, HE KNEW. THEY WOULD MEET AGAIN.

HOGARTH=

TARZAN OF THE APES LIVED ON IN HIS WILD, JUNGLE EXISTENCE WITH LITTLE CHANGE EXCEPT THAT HE GREW STRONGER AND WISER, AND FROM HIS BOOKS LEARNED MORE OF THE STRANGE WORLDS WHICH LAY SOMEWHERE OUTSIDE HIS PRIMEVAL FOREST.

WITH TANTOR THE ELEPHANT HE HAD MADE FRIENDS, AND ON MANY MOONLIT NIGHTS THEY WALKED TOGETHER, OR WHERE IT WAS CLEAR, HE RODE ON TANTOR'S MIGHTY BACK.

THUS, AT EIGHTEEN, WHILE HE COULD READ AND WRITE ENGLISH, TARZAN SPOKE NO HUMAN LANGUAGE -- ONLY THAT OF THE BEASTS -- SINCE HE HAD NEVER SEEN A HUMAN BEING OTHER THAN HIMSELF. SO IT HAPPENED ONE DAY THAT THE SECURITY OF HIS JUNGLE WAS BROKEN FOREVER, WHEN THERE APPEARED A STRANGE CAVALCADE, STRUNG IN SINGLE FILE, OVER THE BROW OF A LOW HILL.

IN ADVANCE WERE FIFTY WARRIORS ARMED WITH SPEARS, LONG BOWS, AND POISONED ARROWS. THEN CAME SEVERAL HUNDRED WOMEN AND CHILDREN BEARING BURDENS AND UTENSILS, AND BEHIND, A LARGE REAR GUARD. IT WAS CLEAR THAT THEY FEARED AN ATTACK. INDEED, THEY WERE FLEEING FROM A FORCE OF SOLDIERS SEEKING VENGEANCE FOR A MASSACRE OF TROOPS WHO HAD HARASSED THEM FOR IVORY.

INTO THE UNTRACKED JUNGLE THEY MARCHED, THIS REMNANT OF A ONCE POWERFUL TRIBE, TOWARD THE UNKNOWN AND FREEDOM. AT A CLEARING NEAR A RIVER THEY SET TO WORK TO BUILD A VILLAGE, ERECTING HUTS AND PALISADES. IN A MONTH THEY HAD TAKEN UP LIFE IN THEIR NEW HOME. HERE THERE WERE NO WHITE MEN, NO SOLDIERS, NO RUBBER OR IVORY TO BE GATHERED FOR CRUEL AND THANKLESS TASKMASTERS.

SEVERAL MOONS PASSED ERE THE BLACKS VENTURED BEYOND THE VILLAGE STOCKADE. BUT ONE DAY KULONGA, THE KING'S SON, WANDERED INTO THE DENSE MAZES OF THE FOREST, EQUIPPED WITH BOW AND POISONED ARROWS, HIS LANCE AND SHIELD READY.

NIGHT FOUND HIM FAR FROM THE VILLAGE; SO HE MADE A RUDE PLATFORM IN A TREE AND CURLED UP TO SLEEP.

THE NEXT DAWN, NEARBY, THE TRIBE OF KERCHAK WAS ASTIR SEARCHING FOR FOOD. TARZAN LEISURELY HUNTED. AND KALA ...

...BUSILY ENGAGED DOWNTRAIL, WAS STARTLED BY A FAINT, STRANGE NOISE. FULL FIFTY YARDS BEFORE HER, SHE SAW THE STEALTHY ADVANCE OF A STRANGE AND FEARSOME CREATURE. IT WAS KULONGA.

KALA TURNED AND
MOVED RAPIDLY BACK
ALONG THE TRAIL.

SHE SOUGHT TO AVOID RATHER THAN ESCAPE. CLOSE AFTER
HER CAME KULONGA. HERE WAS MEAT AND HE WAS HUNGRY.
ON HE HURRIED, HIS SPEAR POISED FOR THE THROW.

AT A BEND IN THE TRAIL,
HIS ARM SHOT BACK. LIGHTNING-
LIKE THE SPEAR SPED TOWARD KALA.

BUT IT GRAZED HER SIDE.
WITH A CRY OF RAGE, SHE
TURNED UPON HER TORMENTOR.

HOGARTH

AS SHE CHARGED, KULONGA UNSLUNG HIS BOW, FITTED AN ARROW AND DROVE THE POISONED MISSLE INTO THE HEART OF THE GREAT ANTHROPOID.

IN THE TREES THE APES SWUNG RAPIDLY TOWARD THE PLACE OF KALA'S HORRID SCREAM. BEFORE THE ASTONISHED MEMBERS OF THE TRIBE, KALA PLUNGED FORWARD ON HER FACE.

ROARING, THEY DASHED TOWARD KULONGA. BUT THE WARY HUNTER WAS DARTING AWAY LIKE A FRIGHTENED ANTELOPE.

TARZAN'S GRIEF AND ANGER WERE UNBOUNDED. HE ROARED OUT HIS HIDEOUS CHALLENGE TIME AND AGAIN . HE BEAT UPON HIS GREAT CHEST WITH HIS CLENCHED FISTS, AND THEN HE FELL UPON THE BODY OF KALA AND SOBBED OUT THE PITIFUL SORROWING OF HIS LONELY HEART. TO LOSE THE ONLY CREATURE IN ALL ONE'S WORLD WHO EVER HAD MANIFESTED LOVE AND AFFECTION FOR ONE IS A GREAT BEREAVEMENT INDEED. WHAT THOUGH KALA WAS A FIERCE AND HIDEOUS APE ! TO TARZAN SHE HAD BEEN KIND, SHE HAD BEEN BEAUTIFUL . UPON HER HE HAD LAVISHED, UNKNOWN TO HIMSELF, ALL THE REVERENCE AND RESPECT AND LOVE THAT A NORMAL ENGLISH BOY FEELS FOR HIS OWN MOTHER. HE HAD NEVER KNOWN ANOTHER, AND SO TO KALA WAS GIVEN, THOUGH MUTELY, ALL THAT WOULD HAVE BELONGED TO THE FAIR AND LOVELY LADY ALICE HAD SHE LIVED.

AFTER THE OUTBURST OF GRIEF, TARZAN
QUESTIONED THE MEMBERS OF THE TRIBE
WHO HAD WITNESSED THE KILLING OF KALA.

HE LEARNED ALL THAT THEIR MEAGER VOCABULARY COULD VOUCHSAFE HIM. IT WAS ENOUGH, HOWEVER, FOR HIS NEEDS. IT TOLD
HIM OF A STRANGE, HAIRLESS, BLACK APE WITH FEATHERS GROWING UPON ITS HEAD, WHO LAUNCHED DEATH FROM A SLENDER
BRANCH, AND THEN RAN, WITH THE FLEETNESS OF BARA, THE DEER, TOWARD THE RISING SUN.

TARZAN WAITED NO LONGER, BUT LEAPING INTO THE BRANCHES
OF THE TREES SPED RAPIDLY THROUGH THE FOREST, TO INTERCEPT THE
BLACK WARRIOR WHO WAS EVIDENTLY FOLLOWING THE TORTUOUS DETOURS OF THE TRAIL.

IN AN HOUR HE CAME UPON THE TRAIL.
IN THE SOFT MUD ON THE BANK OF A TINY
RIVULET HE FOUND FOOTPRINTS SUCH AS HE
ALONE IN ALL THE JUNGLE HAD EVER MADE, BUT MUCH
LARGER THAN HIS. HIS HEART BEAT FAST. COULD IT BE
THAT HE WAS TRAILING A *MAN* -- ONE OF HIS OWN RACE ?

HE SPED OFF. BARELY A MILE BEYOND,
HE CAME UPON THE BLACK WARRIOR.
OPPOSITE HIM STOOD HORTA, THE BOAR,
READY TO CHARGE. TARZAN LOOKED WITH
WONDER UPON THE STRANGE CREATURE BENEATH HIM...

... SO LIKE HIM IN FORM
AND YET SO DIFFERENT IN FACE
AND COLOR. HIS BOOKS HAD PORTRAYED
THE *NEGRO*, BUT HOW DIFFERENT HAD BEEN THE
DULL, DEAD PRINT TO THIS SLEEK FIGURE OF EBONY, PULSING WITH LIFE.

HORTA CHARGED AS KULONGA DODGED, AND SENT AN ARROW INTO ITS BACK. THE BOAR STAGGERED -- AND FELL.

TARZAN WATCHED AS KULONGA CUT SEVERAL STRIPS FROM THE BOAR'S BODY, BUILT A FIRE, AND ATE HIS FILL.

TARZAN'S DESIRE TO KILL BURNED FIERCELY IN HIS WILD BREAST, BUT HIS DESIRE TO LEARN WAS EVEN GREATER. HE WOULD FOLLOW THIS STRANGE CREATURE FOR A WHILE AND KNOW FROM WHENCE HE CAME. HE COULD KILL HIM AT HIS LEISURE LATER, WHEN THE BOW AND DEADLY ARROWS WERE LAID ASIDE.

WHEN KULONGA HAD FINISHED HIS REPAST AND
DISAPPEARED BEYOND A NEAR TURNING OF THE
PATH, TARZAN DROPPED QUICKLY TO THE GROUND.
WITH HIS KNIFE HE SEVERED MANY STRIPS OF MEAT FROM
HORTA'S CARCASS, BUT HE DID NOT COOK THEM.

HE HAD SEEN FIRE, BUT
ONLY WHEN ARA, THE
LIGHTNING, HAD
DESTROYED SOME
GREAT TREE.

WHY THE WARRIOR HAD
RUINED HIS DELICIOUS REPAST
BY PLUNGING IT INTO THE
BLIGHTING HEAT WAS QUITE BEYOND
HIM. POSSIBLY ARA WAS A FRIEND WITH WHOM
THE ARCHER WAS SHARING HIS FOOD.

BUT, TARZAN WOULD NOT RUIN GOOD
MEAT IN ANY SUCH FOOLISH MANNER ...

... SO HE GOBBLED DOWN A GREAT QUANTITY OF THE
RAW FLESH, BURYING THE BALANCE OF THE CARCASS BESIDE
THE TRAIL WHERE HE COULD FIND IT UPON HIS RETURN.

THEN TARZAN, LORD GREYSTOKE, WIPED HIS GREASY FINGERS ON HIS NAKED THIGHS AND TOOK UP KULONGA'S TRAIL. ALL DAY TARZAN FOLLOWED THE BLACK WARRIOR.

TWICE HE SAW HIM HURL HIS POISONED ARROWS OF DESTRUCTION. IN EACH INSTANCE THE ANIMAL DIED ALMOST INSTANTLY. THERE WAS SOMETHING WONDROUS IN THE TINY SLIVERS, HE THOUGHT, WHICH COULD BRING DEATH BY A MERE SCRATCH.

HOGARTH

THAT NIGHT KULONGA SLEPT IN THE CROTCH OF A TREE, AND WHEN HE AWOKE, HIS BOW AND ARROWS HAD VANISHED. HE WAS FURIOUS-- AND FRIGHTENED. NOW HE WAS DEFENSELESS EXCEPT FOR HIS KNIFE. AND THERE WAS NO SIGN OF THE MARAUDER.

HIS ONLY HOPE LAY IN REACHING HIS FATHER'S VILLAGE AS QUICKLY AS POSSIBLE. AND IN HIS WAKE SWUNG TARZAN OF THE APES.

KULONGA'S WEAPONS WERE TIED HIGH IN THE TOP OF A TREE FROM WHICH A PATCH OF BARK HAD BEEN REMOVED NEAR TO THE GROUND, AND A HALF CUT BRANCH LEFT HANGING HIGHER UP. THUS TARZAN MARKED HIS CACHE.

HOGARTH

AS KULONGA CAME TO A CLEARING, A SLENDER COIL SPED OUT SINUOUSLY AND A QUICK NOOSE TIGHTENED ABOUT HIS NECK. HIS CRY OF ALARM WAS THROTTLED...

...AS HE SWUNG THRESHING UPWARD INTO THE LEAFY VERDURE. HAND OVER HAND TARZAN DREW HIS STRUGGLING VICTIM.

HE FASTENED THE ROPE SECURELY TO A STOUT BRANCH. THEN DESCENDING, HE PLUNGED HIS KNIFE INTO KULONGA'S HEART. KALA WAS AVENGED.

HE EXAMINED THE BLACK MINUTELY FOR HE HAD NEVER SEEN ANY OTHER HUMAN BEING. HE MARVELED AT THE TATTOOING, THE FILED TEETH; HE ADMIRED HIS DRESS AND GEAR, KNIFE AND SHEATH, AND THESE HE APPROPRIATED.

BUT NOW HE WAS HUNGRY -- AND HERE WAS MEAT, MEAT OF THE KILL.

WAS NOT KULONGA TO BE EATEN AS FAIRLY AS HORTA, THE BOAR, OR BARA, THE DEER? HE HESITATED. DID MEN EAT MEN?

ALAS, HE DID NOT KNOW --
AND THE THOUGHT STAYED HIS HAND. HE LOWERED THE BODY TO THE GROUND.

FROM A LOFTY PERCH TARZAN VIEWED THE VILLAGE OF THATCHED HUTS ACROSS THE INTERVENING PLANTATION. HE SAW THAT AT ONE POINT THE FOREST TOUCHED THE VILLAGE, AND TO THIS SPOT HE MADE HIS WAY, LURED BY A FEVER OF CURIOSITY TO BEHOLD ANIMALS OF HIS OWN KIND, AND TO LEARN MORE OF THEIR WAYS AND VIEW THE STRANGE LAIRS IN WHICH THEY LIVED.

HIS SAVAGE LIFE AMONG THE FIERCE, WILD BRUTES OF THE JUNGLE LEFT NO OPENING FOR ANY THOUGHT THAT THESE COULD BE AUGHT ELSE THAN ENEMIES. SIMILARITY OF FORM LED HIM INTO NO ERRONEOUS CONCEPTION OF THE WELCOME THAT WOULD BE ACCORDED HIM SHOULD HE BE DISCOVERED BY THESE, THE FIRST OF HIS OWN KIND HE HAD EVER SEEN.

TARZAN OF THE APES WAS NO SENTIMENTALIST. HE KNEW NOTHING OF THE BROTHERHOOD OF MAN. ALL THINGS OUTSIDE HIS OWN TRIBE WERE HIS DEADLY ENEMIES, WITH THE FEW EXCEPTIONS OF WHICH TANTOR, THE ELEPHANT, WAS A MARKED EXAMPLE.

AND HE REALIZED ALL THIS WITHOUT MALICE OR HATRED. TO KILL WAS THE LAW OF THE WILD WORLD HE KNEW. FEW WERE HIS PRIMITIVE PLEASURES, BUT THE GREATEST OF THESE WAS TO HUNT AND KILL, AND SO HE ACCORDED TO OTHERS THE RIGHT TO CHERISH THE SAME DESIRES AS HE, EVEN THOUGH HE HIMSELF MIGHT BE THE OBJECT OF THEIR HUNT. HIS STRANGE LIFE HAD LEFT HIM NEITHER MOROSE NOR BLOODTHIRSTY. THAT HE JOYED IN KILLING AND THAT HE KILLED WITH A JOYOUS LAUGH UPON HIS HANDSOME LIPS BETOKENED NO INNATE CRUELTY. HE KILLED FOR FOOD MOST OFTEN, BUT, BEING A MAN, HE SOMETIMES KILLED FOR PLEASURE, A THING WHICH NO OTHER ANIMAL DOES.

AND WHEN HE KILLED FOR REVENGE, OR IN SELF-DEFENSE, HE DID THAT ALSO WITHOUT HYSTERIA, BUT IT WAS A VERY BUSINESSLIKE PROCEEDING.

SO IT WAS THAT NOW, AS HE CAUTIOUSLY APPROACHED THE VILLAGE OF MBONGA, HE WAS QUITE PREPARED EITHER TO KILL OR BE KILLED SHOULD HE BE DISCOVERED. HE PROCEEDED WITH UNWONTED STEALTH, FOR KULONGA HAD TAUGHT HIM GREAT RESPECT FOR THE LITTLE SHARP SPLINTERS OF WOOD WHICH DEALT DEATH SO SWIFTLY AND UNERRINGLY.

HOGARTH=

FROM A GREAT TREE HE LOOKED
WITH WONDER UPON THIS STRANGE NEW LIFE;

HOW THE NAKED CHILDREN PLAYED; HOW THE
WOMEN WORKED AND GATHERED; AND HOW
THE MEN WERE ARMED AND GUARDED THE VILLAGE.

HE OBSERVED A WOMAN STIRRING A CAULDRON OVER A LOW FIRE. IN IT BUBBLED
A THICK, TARRY MASS. NOW AND THEN SHE DIPPED LITTLE ARROWS INTO THE SEETHING
SUBSTANCE WITH GREAT CARE. TARZAN WAS FASCINATED. THIS, HE REASONED, WAS THE DEADLY STUFF THAT KILLED.

HOW HE WISHED FOR MORE OF THESE DEADLY
SLIVERS! IF ONLY THE WOMAN WOULD LEAVE
HER WORK HE COULD DROP DOWN AND GATHER
A HANDFUL. SUDDENLY A WILD CRY CAME
FROM ACROSS THE CLEARING.

A WARRIOR, BENEATH THE VERY TREE IN
WHICH HE HAD KILLED THE MURDERER OF KALA,
WAS SHOUTING AND WAVING HIS SPEAR.

THE VILLAGE WAS IN
AN INSTANT UPROAR.
ARMED MEN RACED
TO THE SCENE.

QUICKLY AND NOISELESSLY TARZAN DROPPED BESIDE THE
DESERTED CAULDRON OF POISON.
NO ONE WAS IN SIGHT.

JUST THEN THE DOORWAY OF A STRANGE HUT
CAUGHT HIS EYE. CAUTIOUSLY HE SLIPPED INSIDE.

IT WAS A ROOM FULL OF WEAPONS -- KNIVES, SHIELDS,
SPEARS ; AND ON THE FLOOR LAY A PILE OF HUMAN SKULLS.

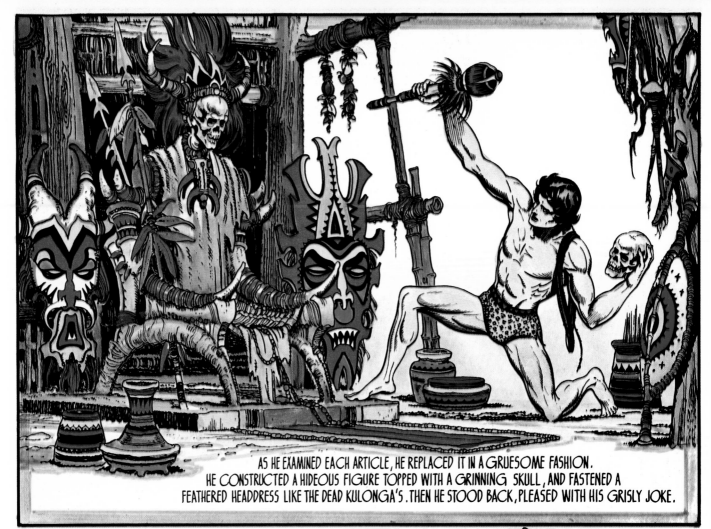

AS HE EXAMINED EACH ARTICLE, HE REPLACED IT IN A GRUESOME FASHION.
HE CONSTRUCTED A HIDEOUS FIGURE TOPPED WITH A GRINNING SKULL, AND FASTENED A
FEATHERED HEADDRESS LIKE THE DEAD KULONGA'S. THEN HE STOOD BACK, PLEASED WITH HIS GRISLY JOKE.

BUT NOW OUTSIDE HE HEARD
THE SOUND OF WAILING. LIKE
A FLASH HE SPED OUT...

...GATHERED UP A HANDFUL OF ARROWS, KICKED OVER
THE CAULDRON, AND LEAPED INTO THE TREES.

IN THE VILLAGE, A PROCESSION FORMED, BEARING THE BODY OF KULONGA WITH LOUD LAMENTATIONS. THEY CAME TO THE HUT WHERE TARZAN HAD BEEN, FOR THIS HAD BEEN KULONGA'S DWELLING.

M'BONGA, THE CHIEF, PEERED IN, AND QUICKLY DREW BACK. THE AWESOME DISCOVERY FILLED HIM WITH DREAD AND SUPERSTITION. FROM AFAR, TARZAN GRINNED.

KALA WAS AVENGED. TARZAN TURNED HOMEWARD TOWARD THE TRIBE OF KERCHAK, STOPPING ONLY TO RETRIEVE KULONGA'S BOW AND ARROWS FROM THE TREE TOP IN WHICH HE HAD HIDDEN THEM.

AMONGST HIS PEOPLE, TARZAN NARRATED
WITH PRIDE THE GLORIES OF HIS ADVENTURE
AND SHOWED THEM HIS SPOILS OF CONQUEST.

KERCHAK TURNED AWAY. SOME DAY HE WOULD
WREAK HIS HATRED ON THIS UPSTART TARZAN.

NOW TARZAN PRACTISED WITH HIS BOW AND
ARROWS. ERE A MONTH HAD PASSED HE WAS NO
MEAN SHOT; BUT LEARNING HIS SKILLS HAD COST
HIM NEARLY HIS ENTIRE SUPPLY OF ARROWS.
SOON HE WOULD HAVE TO REPLENISH THEM.

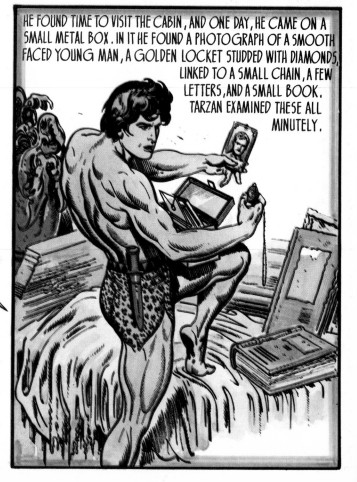

HE FOUND TIME TO VISIT THE CABIN, AND ONE DAY, HE CAME ON A
SMALL METAL BOX. IN IT HE FOUND A PHOTOGRAPH OF A SMOOTH
FACED YOUNG MAN, A GOLDEN LOCKET STUDDED WITH DIAMONDS,
LINKED TO A SMALL CHAIN, A FEW
LETTERS, AND A SMALL BOOK.
TARZAN EXAMINED THESE ALL
MINUTELY.

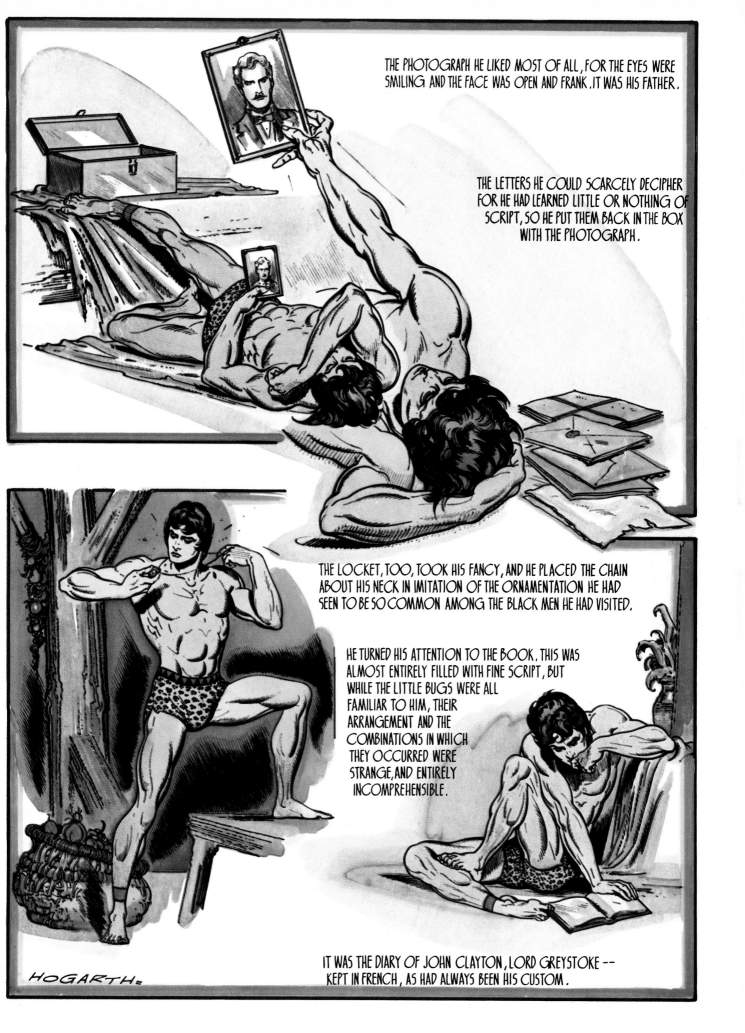

THE PHOTOGRAPH HE LIKED MOST OF ALL, FOR THE EYES WERE SMILING AND THE FACE WAS OPEN AND FRANK. IT WAS HIS FATHER.

THE LETTERS HE COULD SCARCELY DECIPHER FOR HE HAD LEARNED LITTLE OR NOTHING OF SCRIPT, SO HE PUT THEM BACK IN THE BOX WITH THE PHOTOGRAPH.

THE LOCKET, TOO, TOOK HIS FANCY, AND HE PLACED THE CHAIN ABOUT HIS NECK IN IMITATION OF THE ORNAMENTATION HE HAD SEEN TO BE SO COMMON AMONG THE BLACK MEN HE HAD VISITED.

HE TURNED HIS ATTENTION TO THE BOOK. THIS WAS ALMOST ENTIRELY FILLED WITH FINE SCRIPT, BUT WHILE THE LITTLE BUGS WERE ALL FAMILIAR TO HIM, THEIR ARRANGEMENT AND THE COMBINATIONS IN WHICH THEY OCCURRED WERE STRANGE, AND ENTIRELY INCOMPREHENSIBLE.

IT WAS THE DIARY OF JOHN CLAYTON, LORD GREYSTOKE -- KEPT IN FRENCH, AS HAD ALWAYS BEEN HIS CUSTOM.

HOGARTH.

TARZAN REPLACED THE BOX IN THE CUPBOARD, BUT ALWAYS THEREAFTER HE CARRIED THE STRONG, SMILING FACE OF HIS FATHER IN HIS HEART, AND IN HIS HEAD A DETERMINATION TO SOLVE THE MYSTERY OF THE WORDS IN THE LITTLE BLACK BOOK.

AT PRESENT HE HAD MORE URGENT BUSINESS. HIS SUPPLY OF ARROWS WAS EXHAUSTED. HE RETURNED TO M'BONGA'S VILLAGE WHERE A FEAST WAS IN PREPARATION.

THE VICTIM OF THE FEAST WAS A MAN ! AND AS HE WAS DRAGGED TO THE CENTER OF THE VILLAGE, THE WOMEN AND CHILDREN SET UPON HIM WITH STICKS AND STONES. TARZAN WONDERED AT THE CRUELTY OF THESE PEOPLE, AND FROM THAT MOMENT NEVER CEASED TO HOLD HIS OWN KIND IN BUT LOW ESTEEM.

NOW THEY HAD TIED THEIR POOR VICTIM TO A GREAT POST NEAR THE CENTER OF THE VILLAGE, DIRECTLY BEFORE M'BONGA'S HUT, AND HERE THEY FORMED A DANCING, YELLING CIRCLE OF WARRIORS ABOUT HIM, ALIVE WITH FLASHING KNIVES AND SPEARS.

BEYOND SQUATTED THE WOMEN, YELLING AND BEATING UPON DRUMS. IT REMINDED TARZAN OF THE DUM-DUM, AND HE KNEW WHAT TO EXPECT. HE WONDERED IF THEY WOULD SPRING UPON THEIR MEAT WHILE IT WAS STILL ALIVE. THE APES DID NOT DO SUCH THINGS AS THAT.

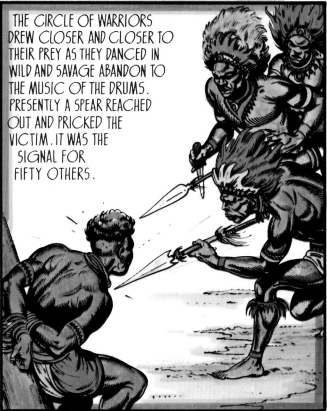

THE CIRCLE OF WARRIORS DREW CLOSER AND CLOSER TO THEIR PREY AS THEY DANCED IN WILD AND SAVAGE ABANDON TO THE MUSIC OF THE DRUMS. PRESENTLY A SPEAR REACHED OUT AND PRICKED THE VICTIM. IT WAS THE SIGNAL FOR FIFTY OTHERS.

WHILE ALL EYES WERE FIXED ON THE THRILLING SPECTACLE, TARZAN SAW HIS CHANCE, GATHERED UP A BUNDLE OF ARROWS AND DEPARTED.

BUT BEFORE HE LEFT, HE HURLED A GRINNING, HUMAN SKULL INTO THEIR MIDST. THE SUDDEN PRESENCE OF THE UNSEEN AND UNEARTHLY EVIL POWER WHICH LURKED ABOUT THEIR VILLAGE SENT THEM INTO A PANIC. THEY BROKE AND RAN.

TARZAN OF THE APES HUNTED AS HE TRAVELED HOMEWARD.

SUDDENLY HE SAW SABOR NOT TWENTY PACES AWAY. THE LIONESS CROUCHED, YELLOW EYES GLEAMING.

TARZAN DID NOT ATTEMPT TO ESCAPE. IN FACT HE WELCOMED THE OPPORTUNITY TO TEST HIS NEW SKILL. QUICKLY HE UN- SLUNG HIS BOW AND FITTED A WELL-DAUBED ARROW.

AS HE DREW THE TAUT BOWSTRING, THE GREAT CAT SPRANG. THE SLIVERED MISSILE LEAPED TO MEET HER IN MID-AIR.

FIRST HE THOUGHT TO REMOVE THE HIDE. RITUALLY HE
ATE OF THE TOUGH, UNSAVORY MEAT OUT OF RESPECT FOR
SABOR. REFRESHED, HE CONTINUED HIS PROGRESS TOWARD THE DOMAIN OF THE APE TRIBE.

WHEN HE FOUND THEM, HE TOLD
OF HIS GREAT EXPLOIT. NOW PROUDLY
HE EXHIBITED HIS TROPHY, THE PELT
OF SABOR, THE LIONESS.

THE TRIBE GATHERED TO LOOK UPON THE PROOF OF HIS WONDROUS PROWESS. ONLY KERCHAK HUNG BACK NURSING HIS HATRED AND RAGE. SUDDENLY SOMETHING SNAPPED IN THE WICKED LITTLE BRAIN OF THE ANTHROPOID.

WITH A FRIGHTFUL ROAR THE GREAT BEAST SPRANG AMONG THE ASSEMBLAGE.

BITING AND STRIKING, HE KILLED AND MAIMED A DOZEN ERE THE BALANCE COULD ESCAPE HIS WRATH.

FROTHING AND SHRIEKING, KERCHAK SAW THE OBJECT OF HIS HATRED ON A NEARBY LIMB. "COME DOWN, TARZAN, GREAT KILLER. COME DOWN AND FEEL THE FANGS OF A GREATER!"

AS THE TRIBE WATCHED
BREATHLESSLY, TARZAN QUIETLY
DROPPED TO THE GROUND.

NEARLY SEVEN FEET STOOD KERCHAK ON HIS SHORT LEGS. HIS LIPS EXPOSED
GREAT FANGS AND HIS EYES SHOT GLEAMS OF MADNESS. AWAITING HIM STOOD TARZAN, ARMED
ONLY WITH HIS KNIFE AND HIS SUPERIOR INTELLECT TO OFFSET THE FEROCIOUS STRENGTH OF HIS ENEMY.

AS THE BRUTE CAME ROARING AT HIM, TARZAN MOVED TO MEET THE ATTACK. WARDING OFF THE ENCIRCLING ARMS---

---HE DODGED, SPRANG IN, AND DROVE THE KNIFE TO THE HILT INTO KERCHAK'S BODY.

BEFORE HE COULD WRENCH THE BLADE FREE AGAIN, THE BULL'S QUICK LUNGE TO SEIZE HIM IN THOSE AWFUL ARMS...

...HAD TORN THE WEAPON FROM TARZAN'S GRASP.

KERCHAK AIMED A TERRIFIC BLOW AT THE APE-MAN'S HEAD WITH THE FLAT OF HIS HAND, A BLOW WHICH, HAD IT LANDED, MIGHT EASILY HAVE CRUSHED IN THE SIDE OF TARZAN'S SKULL.

THE MAN WAS TOO QUICK, AND, DUCKING BENEATH IT, HIMSELF DELIVERED A MIGHTY ONE, WITH CLENCHED FIST, IN THE PIT OF KERCHAK'S STOMACH.

THE APE WAS STAGGERED. DESPITE THE MORTAL WOUND IN HIS SIDE, HE RALLIED IN ONE MIGHTY EFFORT. HE CLOSED UPON THE APE-MAN AND THE GREAT JAWS SOUGHT TARZAN'S THROAT.

BUT THE YOUNG LORD'S SINEWY FINGERS WERE AT KERCHAK'S OWN THROAT BEFORE THE CRUEL FANGS COULD CLOSE ON TARZAN'S SLEEK BROWN SKIN.

THUS THEY STRUGGLED, THE ONE TO CRUSH OUT HIS OPPONENT'S LIFE WITH THOSE AWFUL TEETH, THE OTHER TO CLOSE FOREVER THE WINDPIPE BENEATH HIS GRASP. FOR A WHILE, TARZAN HELD THE SNARLING JAWS FROM HIM. THE GREATER STRENGTH OF THE APE WAS SLOWLY PREVAILING, AND THE FANGS OF THE BEAST WERE CLOSE UPON TARZAN'S THROAT WHEN ...

... WITH A SHUDDERING TREMOR, THE GREAT APE STIFFENED FOR AN INSTANT AND THEN SANK LIMPLY TO THE GROUND. KERCHAK WAS DEAD.

WITHDRAWING THE
KNIFE THAT HAD SO OFTEN
RENDERED HIM MASTER OF
FAR MIGHTIER MUSCLES
THAN HIS OWN, TARZAN OF
THE APES PLACED HIS FOOT
UPON THE NECK OF HIS
VANQUISHED ENEMY, AND ONCE
AGAIN, LOUD THROUGH THE FOREST RANG
THE FIERCE, WILD CRY OF CONQUEROR.

HOGARTH

AND THUS CAME THE
YOUNG LORD GREYSTOKE
INTO THE KINGSHIP OF THE APES.

Edited by Heather Meredith-Owens
Designed by James Craig and Robert Fillie
Set in 12 pt. Bookman by Atlantic Linotype
Printed by Parish Press, Inc.
Bound by Economy Bookbinding Co.